Los Angeles Dodgers 2021

A Baseball Companion

Edited by Steven Goldman and Bret Sayre

Baseball Prospectus

Craig Brown, Associate Editor
Robert Au, Harry Pavlidis and Amy Pircher, Statistics Editors

Copyright © 2021 by DIY Baseball, LLC.
All rights reserved

This book or any part thereof may not be reproduced or transmitted in any form or by any means, electronic or mechanical, including photocopying, recording, or by any information storage and retrieval system, without permission in writing from the publisher.

Limit of Liability/Disclaimer of Warranty: While the publisher and the author have used their best efforts in preparing this book, they make no representations or warranties with respect to the accuracy or completeness of the contents of this book and specifically disclaim any implied warranties of merchantability or fitness for a particular purpose. No warranty may be created or extended by sales representatives or written sales materials. The advice and strategies contained herein may not be suitable for your situation. You should consult with a professional where appropriate. Neither the publisher nor the author shall be liable for any loss of profit or any other commercial damages, including but not limited to special, incidental, consequential, or other damages.

Library of Congress Cataloging-in-Publication Data:
paperback
ISBN-13: 978-1-950716-51-7

Project Credits
Cover Design: Ginny Searle
Interior Design and Production: Amy Pircher, Robert Au
Layout: Amy Pircher, Robert Au

Baseball icon courtesy of Uberux, from https://www.shareicon.net/author/uberux

Ballpark diagram courtesy of Lou Spirito/THIRTY81 Project, https://thirty81project.com/

Manufactured in the United States of America
10 9 8 7 6 5 4 3 2 1

Table of Contents

Statistical Introduction v

Part 1: Team Analysis
Performance Graphs 3
2020 Team Performance 4
2021 Team Projections 5
Team Personnel 6
Dodger Stadium Stats 7
Dodgers Team Analysis 9

Part 2: Player Analysis
Dodgers Player Analysis 16
Dodgers Prospects 87

Part 3: Featured Articles
Dodgers All-Time Top 10 Players 101
    by Rob Mains

A Taxonomy of 2020 Abnormalities 107
    by Rob Mains

Tranches of WAR 113
    by Russell A. Carleton

Secondhand Sport 119
    by Patrick Dubuque

Steve Dalkowski Dreaming 123
    by Steven Goldman

A Reward For A Functioning Society 127
    by Cory Frontin and Craig Goldstein

Index of Names 131

Statistical Introduction

Sports are, fundamentally, a blend of athletic endeavor and storytelling. Baseball, like any other sport, tells its stories in so many ways: in the arc of a game from the stands or a season from the box scores, in photos, or even in numbers. At Baseball Prospectus, we understand that statistics don't replace observation or any of baseball's stories, but complement everything else that makes the game so much fun.

What stats help us with is with patterns and precision, variance and value. This book can help you learn things you may not see from watching a game or hundred, whether it's the path of a career over time or the breadth of the entire MLB. We'd also never ask you to choose between our numbers and the experience of viewing a game from the cheap seats or the comfort of your home; our publication combines running the numbers with observations and wisdom from some of the brightest minds we can find. But if you *do* want to learn more about the numbers beyond what's on the backs of player jerseys, let us help explain.

Offense

We've revised our methodology for determining batting value. Long-time readers of the book will notice that we've retired True Average in favor of a new metric: Deserved Runs Created Plus (DRC+). Developed by Jonathan Judge and our stats team, this statistic measures everything a player does at the plate–reaching base, hitting for power, making outs, and moving runners over–and puts it on a scale where 100 equals league-average performance. A DRC+ of 150 is terrific, a DRC+ of 100 is average and a DRC+ of 75 means you better be an excellent defender.

DRC+ also does a better job than any of our previous metrics in taking contextual factors into account. The model adjusts for how the park affects performance, but also for things like the talent of the opposing pitcher, value of different types of batted-ball events, league, temperature and other factors. It's able to describe a player's expected offensive contribution than any other statistic we've found over the years, and also does a better job of predicting future performance as well.

The other aspect of run-scoring is baserunning, which we quantify using Baserunning Runs. BRR not only records the value of stolen bases (or getting caught in the act), but also accounts for all the stuff that doesn't show up on the back of a baseball card: a runner's ability to go first to third on a single, or advance on a fly ball.

Defense

Where offensive value is *relatively* easy to identify and understand, defensive value is ... not. Over the past dozen years, the sabermetric community has focused mostly on stats based on zone data: a real-live human person records the type of batted ball and estimated landing location, and models are created that give expected outs. From there, you can compare fielders' actual outs to those expected ones. Simple, right?

Unfortunately, zone data has two major issues. First, zone data is recorded by commercial data providers who keep the raw data private unless you pay for it. (All the statistics we build in this book and on our website use public data as inputs.) That hurts our ability to test assumptions or duplicate results. Second, over the years it has become apparent that there's quite a bit of "noise" in zone-based fielding analysis. Sometimes the conclusions drawn from zone data don't hold up to scrutiny, and sometimes the different data provided by different providers don't look anything alike, giving wildly different results. Sometimes the hard-working professional stringers or scorers might unknowingly inflict unconscious bias into the mix: for example good fielders will often be credited with more expected outs despite the data, and ballparks with high press boxes tend to score more line drives than ones with a lower press box.

Enter our Fielding Runs Above Average (FRAA). For most positions, FRAA is built from play-by-play data, which allows us to avoid the subjectivity found in many other fielding metrics. The idea is this: count how many fielding plays are made by a given player and compare that to expected plays for an average fielder at their position (based on pitcher ground ball tendencies and batter handedness). Then we adjust for park and base-out situations.

When it comes to catchers, our methodology is a little different thanks to the laundry list of responsibilities they're tasked with beyond just, well, catching and throwing the ball. By now you've probably heard about "framing" or the art of making umpires more likely to call balls outside the strike zone for strikes. To put this into one tidy number, we incorporate pitch tracking data (for the years it exists) and adjust for important factors like pitcher, umpire, batter and home-field advantage using a mixed-model approach. This grants us a number for how many strikes the catcher is personally adding to (or subtracting from) his pitchers' performance ... which we then convert to runs added or lost using linear weights.

Framing is one of the biggest parts of determining catcher value, but we also take into account blocking balls from going past, whether a scorer deems it a passed ball or a wild pitch. We use a similar approach—one that really benefits from the pitch tracking data that tells us what ends up in the dirt and what doesn't. We also include a catcher's ability to prevent stolen bases and how well they field balls in play, and *finally* we come up with our FRAA for catchers.

Pitching

Both pitching and fielding make up the half of baseball that isn't run scoring: run prevention. Separating pitching from fielding is a tough task, and most recent pitching analysis has branched off from Voros McCracken's famous (and controversial) statement, "There is little if any difference among major-league pitchers in their ability to prevent hits on balls hit in the field of play." The research of the analytic community has validated this to some extent, and there are a host of "defense-independent" pitching measures that have been developed to try and extract the effect of the defense behind a hurler from the pitcher's work.

Our solution to this quandary is Deserved Run Average (DRA), our core pitching metric. DRA seeks to evaluate a pitcher's performance, much like earned run average (ERA), the tried-and-true pitching stat you've seen on every baseball broadcast or box score from the past century, but it's very different. To start, DRA takes an event-by-event look at what the pitchers does, and adjusts the value of that event based on different environmental factors like park, batter, catcher, umpire, base-out situation, run differential, inning, defense, home field advantage, pitcher role and temperature. That mixed model gives us a pitcher's expected contribution, similar to what we do for our DRC+ model for hitters and FRAA model for catchers. (Oh, and we also consider the pitcher's effect on basestealing and on balls getting past the catcher.)

DRA is set to the scale of runs allowed per nine innings (RA9) instead of ERA, which makes DRA's scale slightly higher than ERA's. Because of this, for ease of use, we're supplying DRA-, which is much easier for the reader to parse. As with DRC+, DRA- is an "index" stat, meaning instead of using some arbitrary and shifting number to denote what's "good," average is always 100. The reason that it uses a minus rather than a plus is because like ERA, a lower number is better. Therefore a 75 DRA- describes a performance 25 percent better than average, whereas a 150 DRA- means that either a pitcher is getting extremely lucky with their results, or getting ready to try a new pitch.

Since the last time you picked up an edition of this book, we've also made a few minor changes to DRA to make it better. Recent research into "tunneling"—the act of throwing consecutive pitches that appear similar from a batter's point of view until after the swing decision point–data has given us a new contextual factor to account for in DRA: plate distance. This refers to the distance between successive pitches as they approach the plate, and while it has a smaller effect than factors like velocity or whiff rate, it still can help explain pitcher strikeout rate in our model.

Recently Added Descriptive Statistics

Returning to our 2021 edition of the book are a few figures which recently appeared. These numbers may be a little bit more familiar to those of you who have spent some time investigating baseball statistics.

Fastball Percentage

Our fastball percentage (FA%) statistic measures how frequently a pitcher throws a pitch classified as a "fastball," measured as a percentage of overall pitches thrown. We qualify three types of fastballs:

1. The traditional four-seam fastball;
2. The two-seam fastball or sinker;
3. "Hard cutters," which are pitches that have the movement profile of a cut fastball and are used as the pitcher's primary offering or in place of a more traditional fastball.

For example, a pitcher with a FA% of 67 throws any combination of these three pitches about two-thirds of the time.

Whiff Rate

Everybody loves a swing and a miss, and whiff rate (Whiff%) measures how frequently pitchers induce a swinging strike. To calculate Whiff%, we add up all the pitches thrown that ended with a swinging strike, then divide that number by a pitcher's total pitches thrown. Most often, high whiff rates correlate with high strikeout rates (and overall effective pitcher performance).

Called Strike Probability

Called Strike Probability (CSP) is a number that represents the likelihood that all of a pitcher's pitches will be called a strike while controlling for location, pitcher and batter handedness, umpire and count. Here's how it works: on each pitch, our model determines how many times (out of 100) that a similar pitch was called for a strike given those factors mentioned above, and when normalized for each batter's strike zone. Then we average the CSP for all pitches thrown by a pitcher in a season, and that gives us the yearly CSP percentage you see in the stats boxes.

As you might imagine, pitchers with a higher CSP are more likely to work in the zone, where pitchers with a lower CSP are likely locating their pitches outside the normal strike zone, for better or for worse.

Projections

Many of you aren't turning to this book just for a look at what a player has done, but for a look at what a player is going to do: the PECOTA projections. PECOTA, initially developed by Nate Silver (who has moved on to greater fame as a political analyst), consists of three parts:

1. Major-league equivalencies, which use minor-league statistics to project how a player will perform in the major leagues;
2. Baseline forecasts, which use weighted averages and regression to the mean to estimate a player's current true talent level; and
3. Aging curves, which uses the career paths of comparable players to estimate how a player's statistics are likely to change over time.

With all those important things covered, let's take a look at what's in the book this year.

Team Prospectus

Most of this book is composed of team chapters, with one for each of the 30 major-league franchises. On the first page of each chapter, you'll see a box that contains some of the key statistics for each team as well as a very inviting stadium diagram.

We start with the team name, their unadjusted 2020 win-loss record, and their divisional ranking. Beneath that are a host of other team statistics. **Pythag** presents an adjusted 2020 winning percentage, calculated by taking runs scored per game (**RS/G**) and runs allowed per game (**RA/G**) for the team, and running them through a version of Bill James' Pythagorean formula that was refined and improved by David Smyth and Brandon Heipp. (The formula is called "Pythagenpat," which is equally fun to type and to say.)

Next up is **DRC+**, described earlier, to indicate the overall hitting ability of the team either above or below league-average. Run prevention on the pitching side is covered by **DRA** (also mentioned earlier) and another metric: Fielding Independent Pitching (**FIP**), which calculates another ERA-like statistic based on strikeouts, walks, and home runs recorded. Defensive Efficiency Rating (**DER**) tells us the percentage of balls in play turned into outs for the team, and is a quick fielding shorthand that rounds out run prevention.

After that, we have several measures related to roster composition, as opposed to on-field performance. **B-Age** and **P-Age** tell us the average age of a team's batters and pitchers, respectively. **Payroll** is the combined team payroll for all on-field players, and Doug Pappas' Marginal Dollars per Marginal Win (**M$/MW**) tells us how much money a team spent to earn production above replacement level.

Next to each of these stats, we've listed each team's MLB rank in that category from first to 30th. In this, first always indicates a positive outcome and 30th a negative outcome, except in the case of salary—first is highest.

After the franchise statistics, we share a few items about the team's home ballpark. There's the aforementioned diagram of the park's dimensions (including distances to the outfield wall), a graphic showing the height of the wall from the left-field pole to the right-field pole, and a table showing three-year park factors for the stadium. The park factors are displayed as indexes where 100 is average, 110 means that the park inflates the statistic in question by 10 percent, and 90 means that the park deflates the statistic in question by 10 percent.

On the second page of each team chapter, you'll find three graphs. The first is **Payroll History** and helps you see how the team's payroll has compared to the MLB and divisional average payrolls over time. Payroll figures are current as of January 1, 2021; with so many free agents still unsigned as of this writing, the final 2021 figure will likely be significantly different for many teams. (In the meantime, you can always find the most current data at Baseball Prospectus' Cot's Baseball Contracts page.)

The second graph is **Future Commitments** and helps you see the team's future outlays, if any.

The third graph is **Farm System Ranking** and displays how the Baseball Prospectus prospect team has ranked the organization's farm system since 2007.

After the graphs, we have a **Personnel** section that lists many of the important decision-makers and upper-level field and operations staff members for the franchise, as well as any former Baseball Prospectus staff members who are currently part of the organization. (In very rare circumstances, someone might be on both lists!)

Position Players

After all that information and a thoughtful bylined essay covering each team, we present our player comments. These are also bylined, but due to frequent franchise shifts during the offseason, our bylines are more a rough guide than a perfect accounting of who wrote what.

Each player is listed with the major-league team that employed him as of early January 2021. If a player changed teams after that point via free agency, trade, or any other method, you'll be able to find them in the chapter for their previous squad.

As an example, take a look at the player comment for Padres shortstop Fernando Tatis Jr.: the stat block that accompanies his written comment is at the top of this page. First we cover biographical information (age is as of June 30, 2021) before moving onto the stats themselves. Our statistic columns include standard identifying information like **YEAR**, **TEAM**, **LVL** (level of affiliated play) and **AGE** before getting into the numbers. Next, we provide raw, untranslated

Fernando Tatis Jr. SS

Born: 01/02/99 Age: 22 Bats: R Throws: R
Height: 6'3" Weight: 217 Origin: International Free Agent, 2015

YEAR	TEAM	LVL	AGE	PA	R	2B	3B	HR	RBI	BB	K	SB	CS	AVG/OBP/SLG
2018	SA	AA	19	394	77	22	4	16	43	33	109	16	5	.286/.355/.507
2019	SD	MLB	20	372	61	13	6	22	53	30	110	16	6	.317/.379/.590
2020	SD	MLB	21	257	50	11	2	17	45	27	61	11	3	.277/.366/.571
2021 FS	SD	MLB	22	600	95	24	4	31	81	50	165	17	8	.263/.331/.499
2021 DC	SD	MLB	22	628	100	25	4	32	85	53	173	19	8	.263/.331/.499

Comparables: Darryl Strawberry, Bo Bichette, Ronald Acuña Jr.

YEAR	TEAM	LVL	AGE	PA	DRC+	BABIP	BRR	FRAA	WARP
2018	SA	AA	19	394	136	.370	3.0	SS(83): -1.9	2.4
2019	SD	MLB	20	372	118	.410	7.1	SS(83): 0.9	3.4
2020	SD	MLB	21	257	126	.306	0.7	SS(57): -5.5	0.9
2021 FS	SD	MLB	22	600	126	.318	1.7	SS -1	3.9
2021 DC	SD	MLB	22	628	126	.318	1.8	SS -1	4.0

numbers like you might find on the back of your dad's baseball cards: **PA** (plate appearances), **R** (runs), **2B** (doubles), **3B** (triples), **HR** (home runs), **RBI** (runs batted in), **BB** (walks), **K** (strikeouts), **SB** (stolen bases) and **CS** (caught stealing).

Following the basic stats is **Whiff%** (whiff rate), which denotes how often, when a batter swings, he fails to make contact with the ball. Another way to think of this number is an inverse of a hitter's contact rate.

Next, we have unadjusted "slash" statistics: **AVG** (batting average), **OBP** (on-base percentage) and **SLG** (slugging percentage). Following the slash line is **DRC+** (Deserved Runs Created Plus), which we described earlier as total offensive expected contribution compared to the league average.

BABIP (batting average on balls in play) tells us how often a ball in play fell for a hit, and can help us identify whether a batter may have been lucky or not … but note that high BABIPs also tend to follow the great hitters of our time, as well as speedy singles hitters who put the ball on the ground.

The next item is **BRR** (Baserunning Runs), which covers all of a player's baserunning accomplishments including (but not limited to) swiped bags and failed attempts. Next is **FRAA** (Fielding Runs Above Average), which also includes the number of games previously played at each position noted in parentheses. Multi-position players have only their two most frequent positions listed here, but their total FRAA number reflects all positions played.

Our last column here is **WARP** (Wins Above Replacement Player). WARP estimates the total value of a player, which means for hitters it takes into account hitting runs above average (calculated using the DRC+ model), BRR and FRAA. Then, it makes an adjustment for positions played and gives the player a credit

Los Angeles Dodgers 2021

for plate appearances based upon the difference between "replacement level"—which is derived from the quality of players added to a team's roster after the start of the season–and the league average.

The final line just below the stats box is **PECOTA** data, which is discussed further in a following section.

Catchers

Catchers are a special breed, and thus they have earned their own separate box which displays some of the defensive metrics that we've built just for them. As an example, let's check out Yasmani Grandal.

YEAR	TEAM	P. COUNT	FRM RUNS	BLK RUNS	THRW RUNS	TOT RUNS
2018	LAD	16816	15.7	0.8	0.1	16.5
2019	MIL	18740	19.4	1.8	-0.1	21.1
2020	CHW	4830	3.7	0.3	-0.2	3.8
2021	CHW	14430	16.7	-0.6	1.0	17.1
2021	CHW	14430	16.7	0.4	1.0	18.0

The **YEAR** and **TEAM** columns match what you'd find in the other stat box. **P. COUNT** indicates the number of pitches thrown while the catcher was behind the plate, including swinging strikes, fouls and balls in play. **FRM RUNS** is the total run value the catcher provided (or cost) his team by influencing the umpire to call strikes where other catchers did not. **BLK RUNS** expresses the total run value above or below average for the catcher's ability to prevent wild pitches and passed balls. **THRW RUNS** is calculated using a similar model as the previous two statistics, and it measures a catcher's ability to throw out basestealers but also to dissuade them from testing his arm in the first place. It takes into account factors like the pitcher (including his delivery and pickoff move) and baserunner (who could be as fast as Billy Hamilton or as slow as Yonder Alonso). **TOT RUNS** is the sum of all of the previous three statistics.

Pitchers

Let's give our pitchers a turn, using 2020 AL Cy Young winner Shane Bieber as our example. Take a look at his stat block: the first line and the **YEAR**, **TEAM**, **LVL** and **AGE** columns are the same as in the position player example earlier.

Here too, we have a series of columns that display raw, unadjusted statistics compiled by the pitcher over the course of a season: **W** (wins), **L** (losses), **SV** (saves), **G** (games pitched), **GS** (games started), **IP** (innings pitched), **H** (hits allowed) and **HR** (home runs allowed). Next we have two statistics that are rates: **BB/9** (walks per nine innings) and **K/9** (strikeouts per nine innings), before returning to the unadjusted **K** (strikeouts).

Next up is **GB%** (ground ball percentage), which is the percentage of all batted balls that were hit on the ground, including both outs and hits. Remember, this is based on observational data and subject to human error, so please approach this with a healthy dose of skepticism.

BABIP (batting average on balls in play) is calculated using the same methodology as it is for position players, but it often tells us more about a pitcher than it does a hitter. With pitchers, a high BABIP is often due to poor defense or bad luck, and can often be an indicator of potential rebound, and a low BABIP may be cause to expect performance regression. (A typical league-average BABIP is close to .290-.300.)

The metrics **WHIP** (walks plus hits per inning pitched) and **ERA** (earned run average) are old standbys: WHIP measures walks and hits allowed on a per-inning basis, while ERA measures earned runs on a nine-inning basis. Neither of these stats are translated or adjusted.

DRA- (Deserved Run Average) was described at length earlier, and measures how the pitcher "deserved" to perform compared to other pitchers. Please note that since we lack all the data points that would make for a "real" DRA for minor-league events, the DRA- displayed for minor league partial-seasons is based off of different data. (That data is a modified version of our cFIP metric, which you can find more information about on our website.)

Shane Bieber   RHP

Born: 05/31/95   Age: 26   Bats: R   Throws: R
Height: 6'3"   Weight: 200   Origin: Round 4, 2016 Draft (#122 overall)

YEAR	TEAM	LVL	AGE	W	L	SV	G	GS	IP	H	HR	BB/9	K/9	K	GB%	BABIP
2018	AKR	AA	23	3	0	0	5	5	31	26	1	0.3	8.7	30	47.3%	.278
2018	COL	AAA	23	3	1	0	8	8	48^2	30	3	1.1	8.7	47	52.0%	.227
2018	CLE	MLB	23	11	5	0	20	19	114^2	130	13	1.8	9.3	118	46.2%	.356
2019	CLE	MLB	24	15	8	0	34	33	214^1	186	31	1.7	10.9	259	44.4%	.298
2020	CLE	MLB	25	8	1	0	12	12	77^1	46	7	2.4	14.2	122	48.4%	.267
2021 FS	CLE	MLB	26	10	6	0	26	26	150	121	18	2.1	11.7	195	45.5%	.297
2021 DC	CLE	MLB	26	14	7	0	30	30	196.7	159	24	2.1	11.7	257	45.5%	.297

Comparables: Luis Severino, Danny Salazar, Joe Musgrove

YEAR	TEAM	LVL	AGE	WHIP	ERA	DRA-	WARP	MPH	FB%	WHF	CSP
2018	AKR	AA	23	0.87	1.16	61	0.9				
2018	COL	AAA	23	0.74	1.66	69	1.2				
2018	CLE	MLB	23	1.33	4.55	74	2.6	94.7	57.4%	26.2%	
2019	CLE	MLB	24	1.05	3.28	75	4.9	94.4	45.8%	30.8%	
2020	CLE	MLB	25	0.87	1.63	53	2.6	95.3	53.6%	40.7%	
2021 FS	CLE	MLB	26	1.04	2.44	64	4.4	94.7	50.0%	33.2%	44.2%
2021 DC	CLE	MLB	26	1.04	2.44	64	5.8	94.7	50.0%	33.2%	44.2%

Just like with hitters, **WARP** (Wins Above Replacement Player) is a total value metric that puts pitchers of all stripes on the same scale as position players. We use DRA as the primary input for our calculation of WARP. You might notice that relief pitchers (due to their limited innings) may have a lower WARP than you were expecting or than you might see in other WARP-like metrics. WARP does not take leverage into account, just the actions a pitcher performs and the expected value of those actions ... which ends up judging high-leverage relief pitchers differently than you might imagine given their prestige and market value.

MPH gives you the pitcher's 95th percentile velocity for the noted season, in order to give you an idea of what the *peak* fastball velocity a pitcher possesses. Since this comes from our pitch-tracking data, it is not publicly available for minor-league pitchers.

Finally, we display the three new pitching metrics we described earlier. **FB%** (fastball percentage) gives you the percentage of fastballs thrown out of all pitches. **WHF** (whiff rate) tells you the percentage of swinging strikes induced out of all pitches. **CSP** (called strike probability) expresses the likelihood of all pitches thrown to result in a called strike, after controlling for factors like handedness, umpire, pitch type, count and location.

PECOTA

All players have PECOTA projections for 2021, as well as a set of other numbers that describe the performance of comparable players according to PECOTA. All projections for 2021 are for the player at the date we went to press in early January and are projected into the league and park context as indicated by the team abbreviation. (Note that players at very low levels of the minors are too unpredictable to assess using these numbers.) All PECOTA projected statistics represent a player's projected major-league performance.

How we're doing that is a little different this season. There are really two different values that go into the final stat line that you see for PECOTA: How a player performs, and how much playing time he'll be given to perform it. In the past we've estimated playing time based on each team's roster and depth charts, and we'll continue to do that. These projections are denoted as **2021 DC**.

But in many cases, a player won't be projected for major-league playing time; most of the time this is because they aren't projected to be major-league players at all, but still developing as prospects. Or perhaps a player will provide Triple-A depth, only to have an opportunity open up because of injury. For these purposes, we're also supplying a second projection, labeled **2021 FS**, or full season. This is what we would project the player to provide in 600 plate appearances or 150 innings pitched.

Below the projections are the player's three highest-scoring comparable players as determined by PECOTA. All comparables represent a snapshot of how the listed player was performing at the same age as the current player, so if a

23-year-old pitcher is compared to Bartolo Colón, he's actually being compared to a 23-year-old Colón, not the version that pitched for the Rangers in 2018, nor to Colón's career as a whole.

A few points about pitcher projections. First, we aren't yet projecting peak velocity, so that column will be blank in the PECOTA lines. Second, projecting DRA is trickier than evaluating past performance, because it is unclear how deserving each pitcher will be of his anticipated outcomes. However, we know that another DRA-related statistic–contextual FIP or cFIP–estimates future run scoring very well. So for PECOTA, the projected DRA- figures you see are based on the past cFIPs generated by the pitcher and comparable players over time, along with the other factors described above.

If you're familiar with PECOTA, then you'll have noticed that the projection system often appears bullish on players coming off a bad year and bearish on players coming off a good year. (This is because the system weights several previous seasons, not just the most recent one.) In addition, we publish the 50th percentile projections for each player–which is smack in the middle of the range of projected production—which tends to mean PECOTA stat lines don't often have extreme results like 40 home runs or 250 strikeouts in a given season. In essence, PECOTA doesn't project very many extreme seasons.

Managers

After all those wonderful team chapters, we've got statistics for each big-league manager, all of whom are organized by alphabetical order. Here you'll find a block including an extraordinary amount of information collected from each manager's entire career. For more information on the acronyms and what they mean, please visit the Glossary at www.baseballprospectus.com.

There is one important metric that we'd like to call attention to, and you'll find it next to each manager's name: **wRM+** (weighted reliever management plus). Developed by Rob Arthur and Rian Watt, wRM+ investigates how good a manager is at using their best relievers during the moments of highest leverage, using both our proprietary DRA metric as well as Leverage Index. wRM+ is scaled to a league average of 100, and a wRM+ of 105 indicates that relievers were used approximately five percent "better" than average. On the other hand, a wRM+ of 95 would tell us the team used its relievers five percent "worse" than the average team.

While wRM+ does not have an extremely strong correlation with a manager, it is statistically significant; this means that a manager is not *entirely* responsible for a team's wRM+, but does have some effect on that number.

Part 1: Team Analysis

Performance Graphs

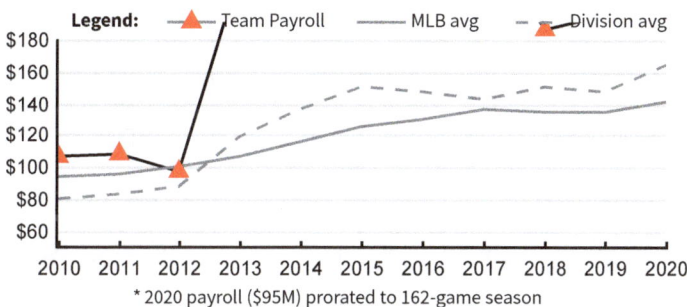

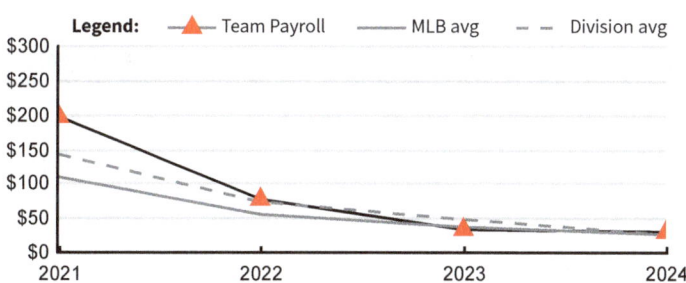

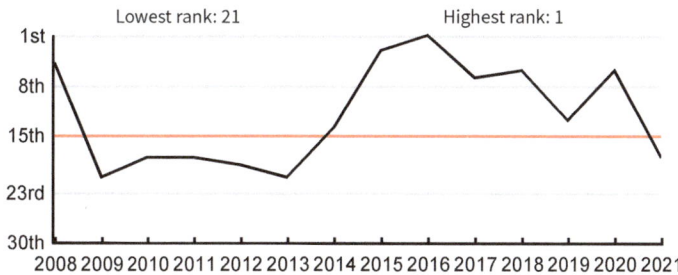

2020 Team Performance

ACTUAL STANDINGS

Team	W	L	Pct
LAD	**43**	**17**	**0.717**
SD	37	23	0.617
SF	29	31	0.483
COL	26	34	0.433
ARI	25	35	0.417

dWIN% STANDINGS

Team	W	L	Pct
LAD	**37**	**23**	**0.624**
SD	34	26	0.567
SF	27	33	0.465
ARI	23	37	0.386
COL	22	38	0.375

TOP HITTERS

Player	WARP
Mookie Betts	2.9
Corey Seager	2.1
Cody Bellinger	1.5

TOP PITCHERS

Player	WARP
Clayton Kershaw	1.3
Tony Gonsolin	0.8
Dustin May	0.8

VITAL STATISTICS

Statistic Name	Value	Rank
Pythagenpat	.719	1st
dWin%	.624	1st
Runs Scored per Game	5.82	1st
Runs Allowed per Game	3.55	2nd
Deserved Runs Created Plus	118	1st
Deserved Run Average Minus	82	1st
Fielding Independent Pitching	3.59	2nd
Defensive Efficiency Rating	.733	2nd
Batter Age	28.6	18th
Pitcher Age	27.6	8th
Payroll	$95.0M	2nd
Marginal $ per Marginal Win	$3.1M	14th

2021 Team Projections

PROJECTED STANDINGS

Team	W	L	Pct	+/-
LAD	104.4	57.6	0.644	-11
With Dustin May ready and David Price returning, adding Trevor Bauer was purely lapidary. Still, they're almost alone in their willingness to put up or shut up.				
SD	95.4	66.6	0.589	-4
Not just Blake Snell, but Yu Darvish and Joe Musgrove; not just Ha-Seong Kim, but Jurickson Profar, all without trading a starting player.				
ARI	79.2	82.8	0.489	11
Mike Hazen is a good trader, but ownership continues to confine him to corner-store bartering.				
SF	74.9	87.1	0.462	-3
Most of their individual moves were small, but the Giants' winter work amounts to the first step toward pivoting from a rebuild to contending.				
COL	58.9	103.1	0.364	-11
The time was ripe for a rebuild, but the return for Nolan Arenado is not a confidence-inspiring start.				

TOP PROJECTED HITTERS

Player	WARP
Mookie Betts	5.6
Cody Bellinger	4.8
Corey Seager	4.0

TOP PROJECTED PITCHERS

Player	WARP
Clayton Kershaw	5.0
Walker Buehler	3.8
Trevor Bauer	3.4

FARM SYSTEM REPORT

Top Prospect	Number of Top 101 Prospects
Josiah Gray, #55	4

KEY DEDUCTIONS

Player	WARP
Joc Pederson	2.5
Alex Wood	1.8
Enrique Hernández	1.4
Pedro Báez	0.7
Dylan Floro	0.7
Adam Kolarek	0.5
Josh Sborz	0.3

KEY ADDITIONS

Player	WARP
Trevor Bauer	3.4
David Price	1.7
Corey Knebel	0.6

Team Personnel

President, Baseball Operations
Andrew Friedman

Senior Vice President, Baseball Operations
Josh Byrnes

Vice President & Assistant General Manager
Jeffrey Kingston

Vice President & Assistant General Manager
Brandon Gomes

Manager
Dave Roberts

BP Alumni
Ricky Conti

Dodger Stadium Stats

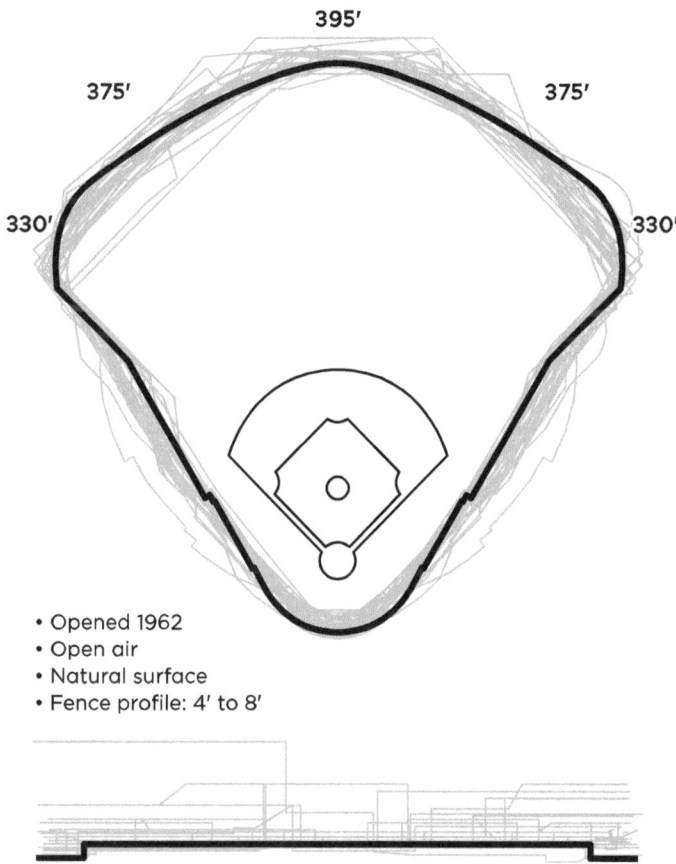

- Opened 1962
- Open air
- Natural surface
- Fence profile: 4' to 8'

Three-Year Park Factors

Runs	Runs/RH	Runs/LH	HR/RH	HR/LH
96	95	100	104	107

Dodgers Team Analysis

In the sixth inning of Game 5 of last October's National League Championship Series, Max Muncy came to the plate to face Braves reliever Will Smith. The Dodgers trailed in the game, 2-1, and in the series, 3-1. Muncy had been an important and emblematic figure in the team's run of success throughout the late 2010s—a former Quad-A anonym who, washing ashore on the paradise island of the Dodger lineup, had transformed himself into one of baseball's canniest observers of the strike zone—but L.A. fans would likely have preferred to see someone else up in that spot, with a man on second and two outs. Mookie Betts, maybe, with his ability to steer the game to himself in the biggest moments. Or Corey Seager, who had spent the postseason to that point dispensing homers to every section of empty bleachers. Or even Cody Bellinger, the 2019 NL MVP who had tailed off in 2020 but whose spiraling swing suggested the sort of theatrics the moment called for.

But, no: it was Muncy's turn, so he set up in the box and went to work, assuming a squatty, dorkily prepared left-handed stance. Smith threw five straight sliders, three balls and two strikes, and Muncy let them all pass by. Then Smith went with a fastball, 96 miles per hour, wire-straight and inches from the outside corner, a nearly perfect pitch. Muncy didn't budge at it.

The walk wasn't much—it might easily have ended up one of the many morsels of misplaced hope that amounted to the team's recent playoff history—until it was. Six pitches later, L.A.'s Will Smith, a young catcher with the accelerated readiness common to Dodger youngsters, cracked a home run (on another full count) to left, putting his team up, 4-2. The homer felt different that it would have minutes before, had it not followed Muncy's plate appearance. Taking the lead then would have been just a sample of the semi-random good fortune baseball metes out in games stocked with star players. Doing it this way, via a slow then sudden accumulation of patient baseball, felt something like a parable.

⚾ ⚾ ⚾

Just over a week later, the Dodgers won the World Series. They'd polished off the comeback against Atlanta, with Bellinger getting his moment in Game 7, thwacking the go-ahead homer to center-right and yanking his shoulder out of its socket in the celebration that followed. They took the Series in 6; their pitching matched Tampa Bay's, and their lineup outslugged the Rays'.

Los Angeles Dodgers 2021

A few minutes after the final out, L.A. manager Dave Roberts stepped to a microphone on a podium, plump with pride. "I told you," he said to some semblance of a Dodger crowd, spread at some semblance of proper distance across the ballpark in Arlington, Texas, "this was our year!"

It was the kind of thing managers say at times like those, but it was a little odd to hear nonetheless, and not only because the notion of 2020 being *anybody's* year, even a champion's, didn't quite resolve. Teams with the Dodgers' trajectory—that mercifully break through after a long period of falling short—tend to possess some identifiable difference, a knack or vibe or approach (real or projected) that distinguishes them from their past disappointed selves. But L.A.'s title run was noteworthy for how closely it hewed to the patterns of their failures. They had the same sort of stacked roster and the same measured-to-the-atom approach. They faced the same October turbulence. To frame the championship as an exception was to do the team that won it a disservice. Anyone can catch a run of luck. It's harder for a group to develop itself as best it can, to devise and believe in its principles, and then to wait.

⚾ ⚾ ⚾

Betts, of course, was new, and crucial. He was the Dodgers' best player during the abbreviated regular season and spent the postseason treating games as playgrounds of pure possibility. He draped himself over outfield walls to bring back home runs; he dashed to whichever base he liked. His hitting numbers tumbled at times—these things happen, in October, in Dodger blue—but it hardly mattered. He played in montage, hands-first-sliding into second and lining a homer and smiling at the pitcher whom he'd just saved two earned runs, one sequence bleeding into the next.

The ethos that brought Betts to L.A., though, wasn't new at all. Where other teams hold to certain patterns of team-building, the Dodgers under Andrew Friedman improve any way they can. Some years, this means spotting a figure like Muncy, with a deep-packed seed of a skill. Some years, it's as simple as seeing that a team is willing to part with one of the best players in baseball, and nabbing him up.

The rest of the cast was familiar. Seager, the stolid and sweet-swinging shortstop. Bellinger, a colt of a player, all limbs and joints and jangling speed. Walker Buehler, matching fastballs with anyone, and the scuffed-up sometimes-virtuosos of the L.A. bullpen. And Clayton Kershaw, the fated embodiment of the whole damn stunning mess.

The temptation is to point to what broke differently. Seager put together the best stretch of his career: 22 hits, 11 walks, and eight homers over 18 playoff games. Kershaw reached a truce with the specters that had haunted his postseason career, winning four of his five starts and parceling 37 strikeouts across 30 clenched-teeth innings. Roberts broke his habit of using his bullpen to maximize narrative tension; it was Julio Urías, not Kershaw or Kenley Jansen, who ran the season's last pitch over the inside corner.

Still, a lot stayed the same. Against Atlanta, the reason L.A. trailed in the first place was a familiar mélange of puzzling baseball: loud bats quieting, relievers flinching at big moments, Kershaw offering up a clunker, apparently requisite even in this redemptive year. That they fought back and won seemed more like time-released logic—this is how this team is supposed to play, right?—than freshly discovered verve.

In the World Series, the Dodgers *really* biffed it, turning the last moments of Game 4 into a case against their own title bona fides. Had they lost the series, the sequence—Jansen throwing a toothless cutter, Chris Taylor juggling a routine single in center, Smith bobbling an on-target throw to the plate and gifting the Rays a win—would have become shorthand for the era.

The crucial difference, then, didn't have to do with basic makeup or ineffable championship quality but with something slipperier. You could call this luck, or timing, or just time. Big plays fell into the innings that needed them, from the same players who'd failed in similar spots. It isn't that the Dodgers couldn't win before and now could. It's that they didn't win before, and now did.

⚾ ⚾ ⚾

It's impossible, or at least pointless, to talk or think or write about the Dodgers without talking or thinking or writing about Kershaw. The question of what a World Series means to L.A. is really, What does it mean to him? Many baseball fans felt no small amount of vicarious joy when the last strike was called and he charged the infield, a look of near-hyperventilation on his face. Some surely harbored a little frustration, that Kershaw's very good playoff run hadn't notched up to a level of blazing all-timer excellence. (Wouldn't have been lovely to see him as Series MVP?) But mostly there was relief—visible from Kershaw and his teammates, palpable from more or less everyone else in the baseball universe. "You want to talk about a narrative?" Roberts said in that echoey postgame speech. "How about being a champion? He's a champion forever."

But in his four postseason wins, set opposite a blowout defeat in his lone appearance against Atlanta, Kershaw didn't so much vindicate as clarify himself. His pre-2020 playoff struggles—the shorthand of the doubled ERA never having quite captured the assortment of big asks, bad breaks, and outlier nights that produced it—have widely been taken as a kind of enduring exception, something that didn't square with the evidence of his regular-season excellence. It may be closer to the truth to consider the two records as opposite sides of a coin. Kershaw has been dominant in outcome but never in approach; he's never made the sport look easy. To watch him work, especially with his present-day low-90s fastball and increasingly balky curve, is to be awed by commitment, not virtuosity. He's a distinctly effortful superstar, and the playoffs have had a way of illustrating just how close to failure his usual success lies.

This October presented its usual challenges. Kershaw breezed past the barely qualified Brewers in the Wild Card round—eight innings, 13 strikeouts, a general air of preamble—but the rest was a struggle. In the divisional round, Manny Machado and Eric Hosmer belted back-to-back sixth-inning homers; he left shortly thereafter, clinging to a one-run lead. In the Series opener, which Kershaw started due not to ace's honors but to the quirks of the rotation schedule, he struggled through a 21-pitch first inning before finding his footing. In Game 5 against the Rays, with Kershaw having given up a pair of runs and encountered a few more nervy moments, Roberts pulled him after five and two-thirds. The slider—the pitch that has become, over the back half of his career, his most trustworthy—had seen him through. It came out of his hand as if barbed, biting heavily into the undersides of bats which then chunked ground balls to the L.A. infielders. It was effective but inelegant; each time, it seemed as if it cost something to throw it.

Looking at Kershaw on the mound, you might not have been able to spot much difference between 2020 and the postseasons prior. He had the same sweatlogged hair and wrenching delivery, wore the same expression: one of intense conviction when he let go of a pitch and deep disappointment when it ended up somewhere he didn't intend. He nodded and yelled and set his jaw in familiar patterns. But after Roberts pulled him for what would end up being the last time of his first championship season, cameras found Kershaw and his manager in the dugout, sharing a smile and a hug.

Before, Kershaw's most famous postseason exits followed the template of disappointment building to defeat. Now: tenuous hope, then victory. Those inclined to look for reasons for the shift could find them. Regular-season slippage, from otherworldly to merely excellent, might have unburdened Kershaw of some measure of imposed expectation. Possibly it persuaded Roberts to give him earlier and more compassionate hooks.

But that he remained foundationally the same player, while achieving a different result, reinforced what may be the central lesson of baseball—one more substantial, anyway, than anything to do with managerial decision-making. Do what you can, again and again, let fate fiddle at the margins, and you'll have something new. Two days after Kershaw's last start, the Dodgers had their title, one that seemed to have been owed to them, individually and as a collective, for a good while. Did they deserve it more, in October 2020, than they had in all those well-credentialed and ultimately disheartening Octobers prior? Only in that they'd waited longer to receive it, and remained themselves in the meantime.

—*Robert O'Connell's work has appeared in The Atlantic, the New York Times, the Guardian, Deadspin, Sports Illustrated, and elsewhere.*

Part 2: Player Analysis

Los Angeles Dodgers 2021

PLAYER COMMENTS WITH GRAPHS

Austin Barnes C
Born: 12/28/89 Age: 31 Bats: R Throws: R
Height: 5'10" Weight: 187 Origin: Round 9, 2011 Draft (#283 overall)

YEAR	TEAM	LVL	AGE	PA	R	2B	3B	HR	RBI	BB	K	SB	CS	AVG/OBP/SLG
2018	LAD	MLB	28	238	32	5	0	4	14	31	67	4	3	.205/.329/.290
2019	OKC	AAA	29	104	19	6	0	6	17	14	20	1	1	.264/.375/.540
2019	LAD	MLB	29	242	28	12	1	5	25	23	56	3	0	.203/.293/.340
2020	LAD	MLB	30	104	14	3	0	1	9	13	24	3	0	.244/.353/.314
2021 FS	LAD	MLB	31	600	77	21	1	15	64	72	143	7	4	.226/.332/.364
2021 DC	LAD	MLB	31	189	24	6	0	4	20	22	45	2	1	.226/.332/.364

Comparables: Doug Mirabelli, Hal King, Jerry Goff

It takes an ugly mistake by an opposing pitcher for Barnes to generate much pop. He tried getting more aggressive early in counts in 2020, but it didn't pay dividends. Happily, though, he need not hit much in order to be a valuable part of a club because he's one of the best pitch-framers in baseball. At the plate, he makes up for lousy bat speed by forcing pitchers to throw him strikes (and thereby drawing a fair number of walks). Behind it, he not only keeps the edges of the strike zone open, but makes up for a below-average arm with quick feet and hands.

YEAR	TEAM	P. COUNT	FRM RUNS	BLK RUNS	THRW RUNS	TOT RUNS
2018	LAD	7110	8.3	1.0	-0.1	9.2
2019	LAD	8092	8.5	0.7	-0.2	8.9
2020	LAD	3848	3.1	0.0	0.2	3.2
2021	LAD	7215	8.1	0.7	-0.3	8.5
2021	LAD	7215	8.1	-0.4	-0.3	7.4

YEAR	TEAM	LVL	AGE	PA	DRC+	BABIP	BRR	FRAA	WARP
2018	LAD	MLB	28	238	74	.287	1.1	C(61): 10.0, 2B(19): 0.2	1.5
2019	OKC	AAA	29	104	104	.274	-0.1	C(13): 2.1, 2B(6): -0.3	0.6
2019	LAD	MLB	29	242	78	.248	2.4	C(64): 8.4, 2B(1): 0.1	1.6
2020	LAD	MLB	30	104	92	.323	0.0	C(28): 0.1	0.6
2021 FS	LAD	MLB	31	600	95	.282	0.0	C 20, 2B 0	4.1
2021 DC	LAD	MLB	31	189	95	.282	0.0	C 9	1.5

Austin Barnes, continued

Batted Ball Distribution

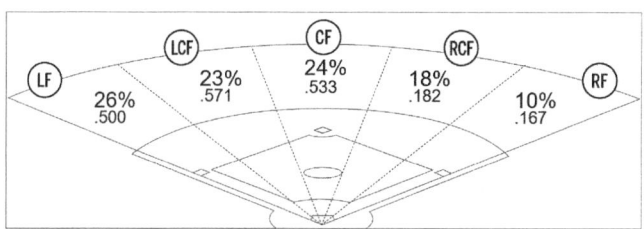

Strike Zone vs LHP   Strike Zone vs RHP

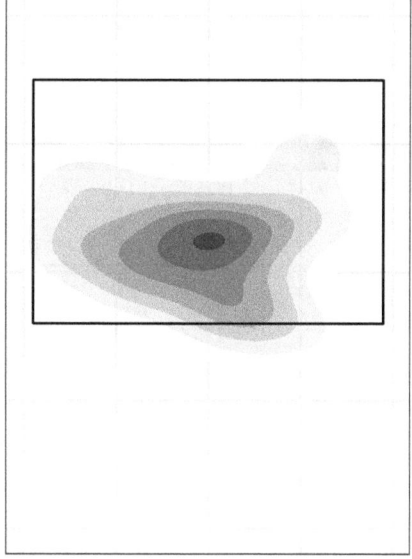

Los Angeles Dodgers 2021

Cody Bellinger CF
Born: 07/13/95 Age: 25 Bats: L Throws: L
Height: 6'4" Weight: 203 Origin: Round 4, 2013 Draft (#124 overall)

YEAR	TEAM	LVL	AGE	PA	R	2B	3B	HR	RBI	BB	K	SB	CS	AVG/OBP/SLG
2018	LAD	MLB	22	632	84	28	7	25	76	69	151	14	1	.260/.343/.470
2019	LAD	MLB	23	661	121	34	3	47	115	95	108	15	5	.305/.406/.629
2020	LAD	MLB	24	243	33	10	0	12	30	30	42	6	1	.239/.333/.455
2021 FS	LAD	MLB	25	600	97	28	2	35	101	75	130	8	3	.266/.363/.530
2021 DC	LAD	MLB	25	604	98	28	2	35	102	76	131	9	3	.266/.363/.530

Comparables: Bob Robertson, Mark McGwire, Fred McGriff

If Tolstoy were alive in 2020, he'd say that good seasons are all alike, but every down year is down in its own way. In 2019, Bellinger and Christian Yelich raced neck-and-neck for the NL MVP award. They were shockingly alike: lanky, powerful, gawkily handsome, graceful, faster than their frames suggest, with swings that appear long but that never seem to miss their targets. Then, in 2020, they both had ugly, frustrating seasons. Their derailments could hardly have been more unequal though. Bellinger mostly hit into bad luck. He had some small swing issues, mishit the ball, and expanded his zone slightly more often, but he continued to draw plenty of walks, rarely struck out, and looked like himself whenever he did get off his 'A' swing. Yelich's troubles are serious. Bellinger's feel like a blip and PECOTA is inclined to agree.

YEAR	TEAM	LVL	AGE	PA	DRC+	BABIP	BRR	FRAA	WARP
2018	LAD	MLB	22	632	112	.312	3.3	1B(110): -0.9, CF(78): 2.0, RF(5): -0.2	2.8
2019	LAD	MLB	23	661	157	.302	0.4	RF(115): 13.3, 1B(36): 1.9, CF(25): 0.1	8.0
2020	LAD	MLB	24	243	117	.245	0.1	CF(39): 4.8, 1B(19): 0.2, RF(1): -0.0	1.5
2021 FS	LAD	MLB	25	600	137	.293	0.1	CF 4, 1B 0	4.6
2021 DC	LAD	MLB	25	604	137	.293	0.1	CF 4, 1B 0	4.8

Cody Bellinger, continued

Batted Ball Distribution

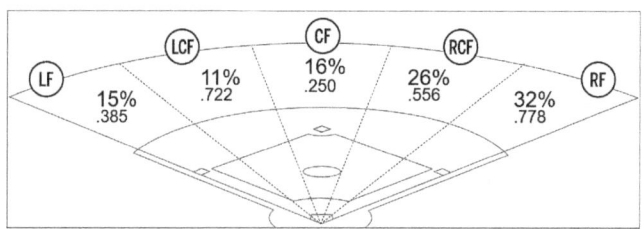

Strike Zone vs LHP   Strike Zone vs RHP

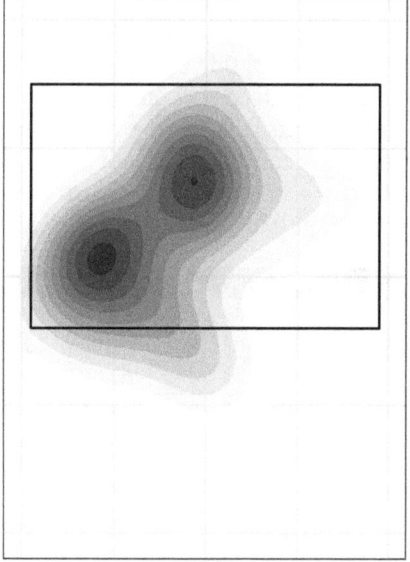

Los Angeles Dodgers 2021

Mookie Betts RF
Born: 10/07/92   Age: 28   Bats: R   Throws: R
Height: 5'9"   Weight: 180   Origin: Round 5, 2011 Draft (#172 overall)

YEAR	TEAM	LVL	AGE	PA	R	2B	3B	HR	RBI	BB	K	SB	CS	AVG/OBP/SLG
2018	BOS	MLB	25	614	129	47	5	32	80	81	91	30	6	.346/.438/.640
2019	BOS	MLB	26	706	135	40	5	29	80	97	101	16	3	.295/.391/.524
2020	LAD	MLB	27	246	47	9	1	16	39	24	38	10	2	.292/.366/.562
2021 FS	LAD	MLB	28	600	107	28	2	31	81	64	94	18	5	.281/.363/.523
2021 DC	LAD	MLB	28	687	122	32	3	36	93	73	108	22	5	.281/.363/.523

Comparables: Jack Clark, Rocky Colavito, Ron Jones

 Betts continues to carve his way into the record books and the ongoing dialogue that is baseball history. When the Red Sox traded him to the Dodgers in February, we had occasion to wonder whether Betts would match the almost vengeful greatness of Frank Robinson after the Reds traded him to Baltimore in 1965. (He basically did.) When Al Kaline died in April, we had a chance to ponder the comparisons thoughtful observers draw between the crisp, intelligent, all-around, all-out game Betts plays, and the way Kaline played at his best. When Betts led the Dodgers' wildcat strike of a game in late August in solidarity with ongoing protests against systemic racism, we were afforded an opportunity to slot him in alongside the other great Black ballplayers who demanded that an unjust world become a bit less so. And throughout this bizarre season, we watched Betts sustain his greatness in a way not even the other players who had been in the conversation with him as the best in the game could match. By all indications, he will remain an extraordinarily well-rounded superstar (on and off the diamond) for another decade.

YEAR	TEAM	LVL	AGE	PA	DRC+	BABIP	BRR	FRAA	WARP
2018	BOS	MLB	25	614	178	.368	3.8	RF(120): 10.7, CF(14): 0.4, 2B(1): 0.0	8.9
2019	BOS	MLB	26	706	137	.309	5.7	RF(132): 11.9, CF(17): 1.6	6.9
2020	LAD	MLB	27	246	150	.289	5.2	RF(52): 4.7, 2B(1): -0.1, CF(1): -0.1	2.9
2021 FS	LAD	MLB	28	600	138	.291	1.0	RF 5, 2B 0	4.9
2021 DC	LAD	MLB	28	687	138	.291	1.1	RF 6	5.6

Mookie Betts, continued

Batted Ball Distribution

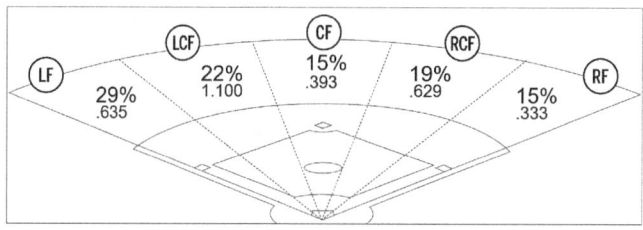

Strike Zone vs LHP   **Strike Zone vs RHP**

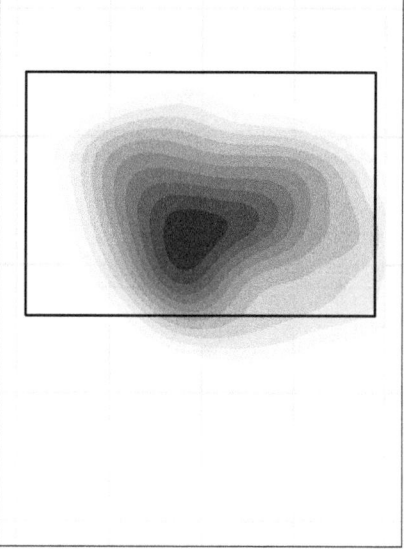

Los Angeles Dodgers 2021

Max Muncy 1B

Born: 08/25/90 Age: 30 Bats: L Throws: R
Height: 6'0" Weight: 215 Origin: Round 5, 2012 Draft (#169 overall)

YEAR	TEAM	LVL	AGE	PA	R	2B	3B	HR	RBI	BB	K	SB	CS	AVG/OBP/SLG
2018	OKC	AAA	27	38	7	2	0	2	4	6	5	0	0	.312/.421/.562
2018	LAD	MLB	27	481	75	17	2	35	79	79	131	3	0	.263/.391/.582
2019	LAD	MLB	28	589	101	22	1	35	98	90	149	4	1	.251/.374/.515
2020	LAD	MLB	29	248	36	4	0	12	27	39	60	1	0	.192/.331/.389
2021 FS	LAD	MLB	30	600	96	24	1	30	86	88	159	2	1	.245/.367/.479
2021 DC	LAD	MLB	30	574	92	23	1	29	83	84	152	2	1	.245/.367/.479

Comparables: Ji-Man Choi, Steve Bilko, Tony Solaita

No one is slump-proof in a 60-game sample. Muncy's 2020 line proves that. Looking past the raw numbers, though, he had another very solid season, generating tons of hard contact, lifting the ball to the pull field, and torturing pitchers with his patience. Had it not been for a pre-season broken finger that remained sore, his results might have better matched those he posted over the two prior campaigns. In the playoffs, he walked 20 times and fanned only 21. Mostly a liability in the field, he nonetheless helped save the season by alerting Clayton Kershaw to an attempted steal of home in the World Series. He's a relentlessly dangerous hitter and a fine baserunner. That makes him a championship-caliber first baseman.

YEAR	TEAM	LVL	AGE	PA	DRC+	BABIP	BRR	FRAA	WARP
2018	OKC	AAA	27	38	131	.320	0.7	1B(7): 0.1, 3B(3): 0.2	0.3
2018	LAD	MLB	27	481	145	.299	2.3	1B(84): -0.5, 3B(38): 0.3, 2B(13): -0.9	3.9
2019	LAD	MLB	28	589	131	.283	4.1	2B(70): -0.1, 1B(65): 4.2, 3B(35): 3.2	5.1
2020	LAD	MLB	29	248	108	.203	0.6	1B(35): -2.6, 3B(16): 1.0, 2B(12): -0.1	0.6
2021 FS	LAD	MLB	30	600	130	.297	-0.8	1B 0, 3B 1	3.5
2021 DC	LAD	MLB	30	574	130	.297	-0.8	1B 0, 3B 1	3.1

Max Muncy, continued

Batted Ball Distribution

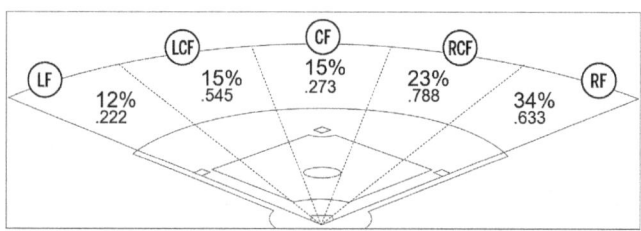

Strike Zone vs LHP   Strike Zone vs RHP

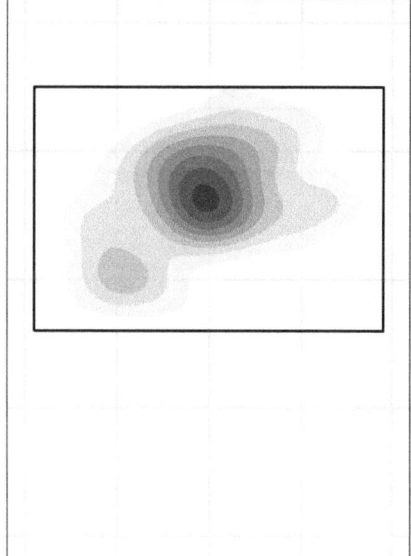

AJ Pollock CF

Born: 12/05/87 Age: 33 Bats: R Throws: R
Height: 6'1" Weight: 210 Origin: Round 1, 2009 Draft (#17 overall)

YEAR	TEAM	LVL	AGE	PA	R	2B	3B	HR	RBI	BB	K	SB	CS	AVG/OBP/SLG
2018	ARI	MLB	30	460	61	21	5	21	65	31	100	13	2	.257/.316/.484
2019	LAD	MLB	31	342	49	15	1	15	47	23	74	5	1	.266/.327/.468
2020	LAD	MLB	32	210	30	9	0	16	34	12	45	2	2	.276/.314/.566
2021 FS	LAD	MLB	33	600	88	25	2	31	92	45	130	17	6	.254/.318/.479
2021 DC	LAD	MLB	33	454	66	19	1	23	69	34	98	12	5	.254/.318/.479

Comparables: Ellis Burks, Carlos Beltrán, Torii Hunter

Without anything material actually changing, Pollock cracked homers at a pace that could have pushed him past 40 had the league played a full 162 games. He's typically an almost frustratingly consistent hitter (that is to say, immune to hot streaks if not injuries), has real power, is still plenty athletic enough to be a plus in left field and seems comfortable in slightly less than a full-time role in which he can stay fresh.

YEAR	TEAM	LVL	AGE	PA	DRC+	BABIP	BRR	FRAA	WARP
2018	ARI	MLB	30	460	106	.284	1.1	CF(109): -7.6	1.3
2019	LAD	MLB	31	342	97	.300	-0.3	CF(62): -8.6, LF(18): -0.1	0.2
2020	LAD	MLB	32	210	121	.277	-0.4	LF(27): -3.1, CF(16): -1.4	0.3
2021 FS	LAD	MLB	33	600	111	.280	1.1	LF -5, CF -1	2.2
2021 DC	LAD	MLB	33	454	111	.280	0.9	LF -4, CF -1	1.4

AJ Pollock, continued

Batted Ball Distribution

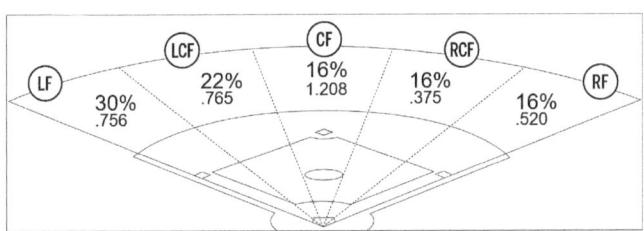

Strike Zone vs LHP   **Strike Zone vs RHP**

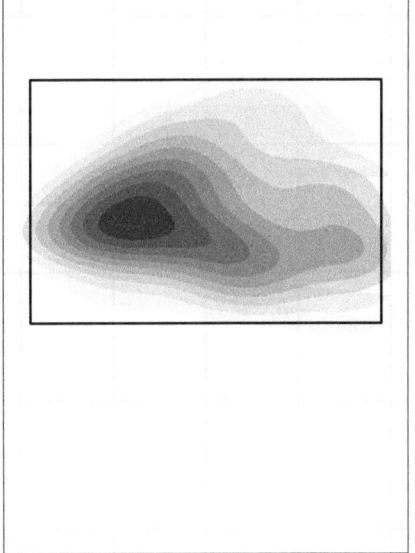

Edwin Ríos 3B

Born: 04/21/94 Age: 27 Bats: L Throws: R
Height: 6'3" Weight: 220 Origin: Round 6, 2015 Draft (#192 overall)

YEAR	TEAM	LVL	AGE	PA	R	2B	3B	HR	RBI	BB	K	SB	CS	AVG/OBP/SLG
2018	OKC	AAA	24	341	45	25	0	10	55	23	110	0	1	.304/.355/.482
2019	OKC	AAA	25	444	72	23	2	31	91	37	153	2	2	.270/.340/.575
2019	LAD	MLB	25	56	10	2	1	4	8	9	21	0	0	.277/.393/.617
2020	LAD	MLB	26	83	13	6	0	8	17	4	18	0	0	.250/.301/.645
2021 FS	LAD	MLB	27	600	77	27	1	25	83	39	188	0	1	.232/.293/.426
2021 DC	LAD	MLB	27	196	25	9	0	8	27	12	61	0	0	.232/.293/.426

Comparables: Zach Green, Zach Lutz, Josh Fields

The flourish of Ríos' high finish after a long, tremendously powerful swing—the way he obviously relishes it, especially when he gets into one and knows it's gone—is a thing of left-handed beauty. The thing is, that's a bit of a left-handed compliment. That swing is never going to generate high contact rates. To sustain the slugging success he's had in the upper minors and limited big-league action, he's going to have to stay aggressive, which means he'll never walk much. He's fringy at third base and likely to be confined to first and/or DH soon. That makes him a risky proposition as a regular, but as a bench bat, he's dangerous in all the right ways.

YEAR	TEAM	LVL	AGE	PA	DRC+	BABIP	BRR	FRAA	WARP
2018	OKC	AAA	24	341	116	.433	-2.4	3B(38): -4.2, 1B(28): -1.3, LF(17): -1.6	0.1
2019	OKC	AAA	25	444	106	.349	-2.6	3B(67): 1.7, 1B(25): 0.6, LF(8): 1.9	1.8
2019	LAD	MLB	25	56	87	.409	-0.2	1B(12): -0.4, 3B(5): -0.5, LF(1): -0.0	-0.1
2020	LAD	MLB	26	83	124	.216	-0.3	3B(21): -1.4, 1B(6): -0.1	0.2
2021 FS	LAD	MLB	27	600	91	.304	-0.9	3B -1, 1B 0	0.2
2021 DC	LAD	MLB	27	196	91	.304	-0.3	3B 0, 1B 0	0.0

Edwin Ríos, continued

Batted Ball Distribution

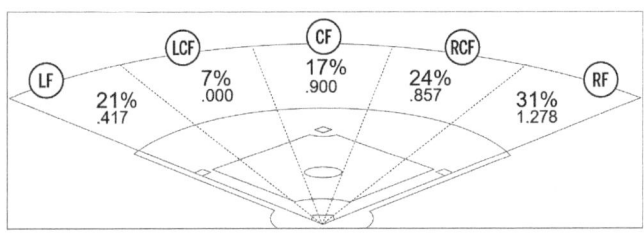

Strike Zone vs LHP   Strike Zone vs RHP

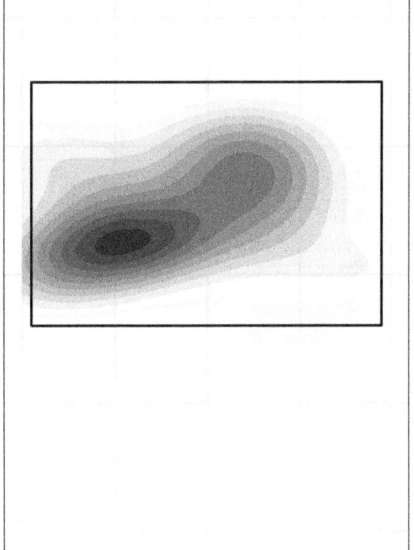

Los Angeles Dodgers 2021

Corey Seager SS
Born: 04/27/94   Age: 27   Bats: L   Throws: R
Height: 6'4"   Weight: 215   Origin: Round 1, 2012 Draft (#18 overall)

YEAR	TEAM	LVL	AGE	PA	R	2B	3B	HR	RBI	BB	K	SB	CS	AVG/OBP/SLG
2018	LAD	MLB	24	115	13	5	1	2	13	11	17	0	0	.267/.348/.396
2019	LAD	MLB	25	541	82	44	1	19	87	44	98	1	0	.272/.335/.483
2020	LAD	MLB	26	232	38	12	1	15	41	17	37	1	0	.307/.358/.585
2021 FS	LAD	MLB	27	600	95	32	2	25	91	53	113	2	2	.284/.355/.494
2021 DC	LAD	MLB	27	617	97	33	2	26	93	55	117	2	2	.284/.355/.494

Comparables: Troy Tulowitzki, Hanley Ramirez, Francisco Lindor

Any list of the most improved hitters of 2020 has to include Seager, and he wasn't bad even before 2020. Extremely aggressive within the zone, but with a swing that generates high contact rates and power to all fields, Seager was the only player in the majors to produce a hard-hit ball (>95 mph) at a launch angle between 0 and 35 degrees in 30 percent of his plate appearances. He's fully healthy for the first time in years, and the serious and studious approach he takes to his craft is beginning to shine through. All of that only became more obvious during the postseason, which he capped off with the World Series MVP award.

YEAR	TEAM	LVL	AGE	PA	DRC+	BABIP	BRR	FRAA	WARP
2018	LAD	MLB	24	115	103	.301	0.8	SS(25): 0.3	0.7
2019	LAD	MLB	25	541	105	.303	0.7	SS(132): 1.2	3.1
2020	LAD	MLB	26	232	138	.309	0.2	SS(43): 4.8	2.1
2021 FS	LAD	MLB	27	600	127	.319	-0.7	SS 1	4.0
2021 DC	LAD	MLB	27	617	127	.319	-0.7	SS 2	4.0

Corey Seager, continued

Batted Ball Distribution

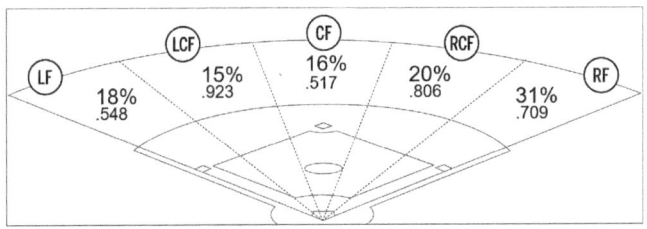

Strike Zone vs LHP   **Strike Zone vs RHP**

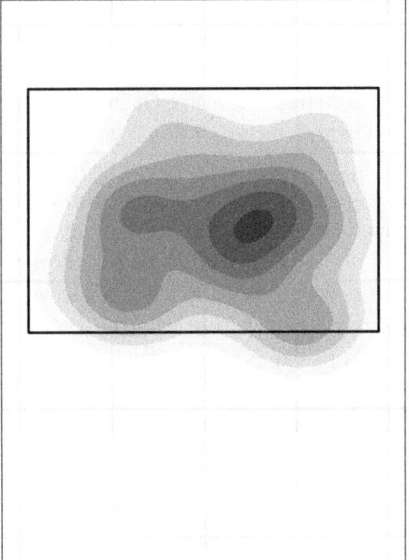

Will Smith C

Born: 03/28/95   Age: 26   Bats: R   Throws: R
Height: 5'10"   Weight: 195   Origin: Round 1, 2016 Draft (#32 overall)

YEAR	TEAM	LVL	AGE	PA	R	2B	3B	HR	RBI	BB	K	SB	CS	AVG/OBP/SLG
2018	TUL	AA	23	307	48	14	0	19	53	36	75	4	0	.264/.358/.532
2018	OKC	AAA	23	98	9	4	0	1	6	7	37	1	0	.138/.206/.218
2019	OKC	AAA	24	270	48	11	2	20	54	40	49	1	0	.268/.381/.603
2019	LAD	MLB	24	196	30	9	0	15	42	18	52	2	0	.253/.337/.571
2020	LAD	MLB	25	137	23	9	0	8	25	20	22	0	0	.289/.401/.579
2021 FS	LAD	MLB	26	600	93	26	1	33	97	66	144	2	1	.253/.352/.503
2021 DC	LAD	MLB	26	466	72	20	1	26	75	51	112	1	1	.253/.352/.503

Comparables: Geovany Soto, Lance Berkman, Tom Haller

Somehow, Smith keeps getting better. It's equal parts easy and impossible to explain: He's just an extremely athletic backstop who has always had solid contact skills and a sound approach, plus good makeup, and once the Dodgers folded him into their state-of-the-art player development machine,

YEAR	TEAM	P. COUNT	FRM RUNS	BLK RUNS	THRW RUNS	TOT RUNS
2018	TUL	4379	7.0	0.1	0.6	7.7
2019	LAD	6644	2.1	1.2	-0.1	3.2
2020	LAD	4351	-1.4	-0.6	0.0	-2.0
2021	LAD	14430	1.6	1.7	0.3	3.6
2021	LAD	14430	1.6	-0.5	0.3	1.3

he launched—literally. Of the 350-odd hitters who had at least 50 batted balls last year, Smith had the seventh-highest average launch angle. Yet he didn't have the attendant problem with popping the ball up that plagues practically every such hitter. He also did so while making more contact because his plate discipline went from quite good to exceptional. The only bad news was behind the plate, where Smith no longer looks like the difference-maker he once projected to be. Still, there's a word for a fringe-average defensive catcher who carries Justin Turner's batted-ball profile, controls the zone like Carlos Santana, and runs like Bo Bichette: superstar.

YEAR	TEAM	LVL	AGE	PA	DRC+	BABIP	BRR	FRAA	WARP
2018	TUL	AA	23	307	131	.295	-1.8	C(33): 7.4, 3B(33): -1.3	2.0
2018	OKC	AAA	23	98	7	.216	1.4	C(16): 1.4, 3B(10): 0.3	-0.4
2019	OKC	AAA	24	270	137	.253	0.9	C(52): -0.1, 3B(1): -0.1	2.5
2019	LAD	MLB	24	196	122	.264	-0.6	C(46): 4.5	1.9
2020	LAD	MLB	25	137	151	.294	-1.3	C(34): 0.3	1.0
2021 FS	LAD	MLB	26	600	129	.288	-0.7	C 4, 3B 0	4.8
2021 DC	LAD	MLB	26	466	129	.288	-0.5	C 4	3.9

Will Smith, continued

Batted Ball Distribution

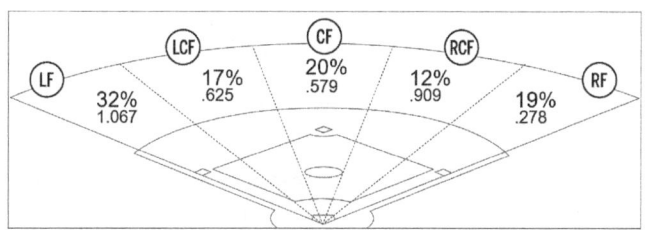

Strike Zone vs LHP   Strike Zone vs RHP

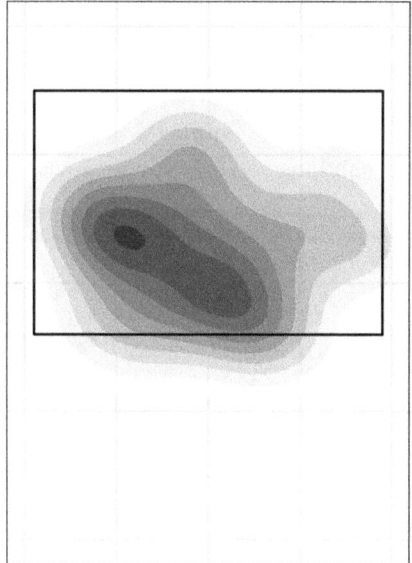

Chris Taylor LF

Born: 08/29/90 Age: 30 Bats: R Throws: R
Height: 6'1" Weight: 196 Origin: Round 5, 2012 Draft (#161 overall)

YEAR	TEAM	LVL	AGE	PA	R	2B	3B	HR	RBI	BB	K	SB	CS	AVG/OBP/SLG
2018	LAD	MLB	27	604	85	35	8	17	63	55	178	9	6	.254/.331/.444
2019	LAD	MLB	28	414	52	29	4	12	52	37	115	8	0	.262/.333/.462
2020	LAD	MLB	29	214	30	10	2	8	32	26	55	3	2	.270/.366/.476
2021 FS	LAD	MLB	30	600	78	23	4	19	75	61	168	11	5	.242/.327/.415
2021 DC	LAD	MLB	30	476	62	18	3	15	59	49	133	8	4	.242/.327/.415

Comparables: Brad Miller, Woodie Held, Jose Valentin

You won't hear most youth coaches recommend wrestling as a companion sport for an aspiring baseball player, save perhaps a catcher, but there's something to it. Wrestlers develop the special relationship with the ground that any elite athlete needs, but which can be especially relevant to baseball. They quickly develop a fine understanding of the application of leverage. Taylor, who comes from a wrestling family, is proof of these things. He's an expert in his own swing, having sought the help of the best swing technicians in the country and used their advice to find improbable power. Generating that pop required some movements that led to a lot of whiffs, so in 2020, he quieted a few things and made more consistent contact. Speaking of leverage, he remains an impressively sterling performer (in the field and in the batter's box) in big moments—both during the regular season and the postseason, even if that's not the first thing you recall about Taylor this year.

YEAR	TEAM	LVL	AGE	PA	DRC+	BABIP	BRR	FRAA	WARP
2018	LAD	MLB	27	604	102	.345	0.9	SS(81): 3.7, CF(50): -4.5, LF(24): 1.5	2.7
2019	LAD	MLB	28	414	91	.344	3.0	LF(56): 0.8, SS(39): -4.6, 2B(20): -1.9	0.8
2020	LAD	MLB	29	214	107	.344	0.3	SS(20): -0.0, LF(19): 0.5, 2B(13): 1.2	1.0
2021 FS	LAD	MLB	30	600	102	.316	0.8	LF 3, CF 0	2.1
2021 DC	LAD	MLB	30	476	102	.316	0.7	LF 2, CF 0	1.6

Chris Taylor, continued

Batted Ball Distribution

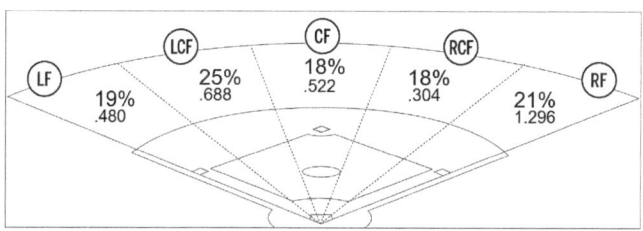

Strike Zone vs LHP

Strike Zone vs RHP

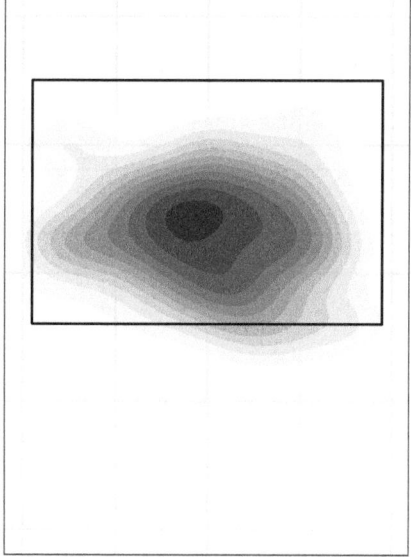

Justin Turner 3B

Born: 11/23/84 Age: 36 Bats: R Throws: R
Height: 5'11" Weight: 202 Origin: Round 7, 2006 Draft (#204 overall)

YEAR	TEAM	LVL	AGE	PA	R	2B	3B	HR	RBI	BB	K	SB	CS	AVG/OBP/SLG
2018	LAD	MLB	33	426	62	31	1	14	52	47	54	2	1	.312/.406/.518
2019	LAD	MLB	34	549	80	24	0	27	67	51	88	2	0	.290/.372/.509
2020	LAD	MLB	35	175	26	9	1	4	23	18	26	1	0	.307/.400/.460
2021 FS	LAD	MLB	36	600	75	25	1	23	78	57	106	4	2	.269/.361/.455
2021 DC	LAD	MLB	36	584	73	25	1	22	76	55	103	4	2	.269/.361/.455

Comparables: Mike Lowell, Douglas DeCinces, Aramis Ramirez

Winter is coming for one of the great early adopters of the fly-ball revolution. He's still exceptionally disciplined at the plate, but more of Turner's swings are coming up empty when he does expand the zone (as is inevitable). He's still a solid third baseman, but the stocky athleticism that once made him a great defender is fading. A hamstring strain shortened his short season. Yet through a thousand changes to his stance, setup and body, Turner has remained impressively constant in terms of profile and production. He'll keep a high floor, even as his decline continues.

YEAR	TEAM	LVL	AGE	PA	DRC+	BABIP	BRR	FRAA	WARP
2018	LAD	MLB	33	426	146	.334	0.3	3B(96): 11.1	5.1
2019	LAD	MLB	34	549	133	.304	-1.3	3B(124): 2.2, 2B(1): -0.0	4.5
2020	LAD	MLB	35	175	133	.347	-1.4	3B(32): 2.6	1.1
2021 FS	LAD	MLB	36	600	124	.298	-0.6	3B 3, 2B 0	3.3
2021 DC	LAD	MLB	36	584	124	.298	-0.6	3B 3	3.2

Justin Turner, continued

Batted Ball Distribution

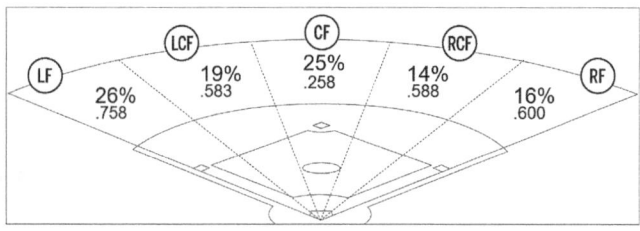

Strike Zone vs LHP   Strike Zone vs RHP

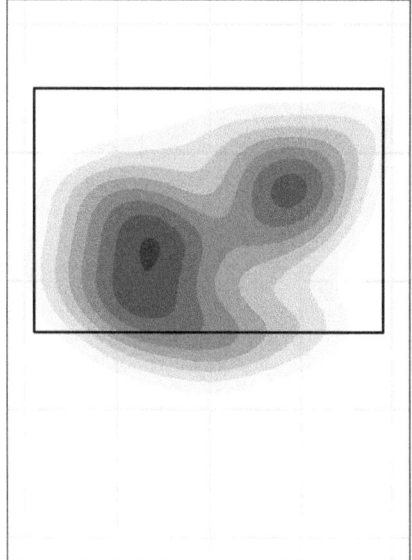

Los Angeles Dodgers 2021

Scott Alexander LHP
Born: 07/10/89 Age: 31 Bats: L Throws: L
Height: 6'2" Weight: 195 Origin: Round 6, 2010 Draft (#179 overall)

YEAR	TEAM	LVL	AGE	W	L	SV	G	GS	IP	H	HR	BB/9	K/9	K	GB%	BABIP
2018	LAD	MLB	28	2	1	3	73	1	66	57	4	3.7	7.6	56	71.0%	.298
2019	LAD	MLB	29	3	2	0	28	0	17¹	17	2	3.6	4.7	9	61.0%	.263
2020	LAD	MLB	30	2	0	0	13	0	12¹	9	2	6.6	6.6	9	67.6%	.226
2021 FS	LAD	MLB	31	2	2	0	57	0	50	47	5	3.9	7.5	41	63.8%	.289
2021 DC	LAD	MLB	31	1	1	0	33	0	49.7	47	5	3.9	7.5	41	63.8%	.289

Comparables: Dan Jennings, Andrew Kittredge, Heath Hembree

His sinker still burns worms, but Alexander's inability to throw his slider for strikes threatens to leave him snakebitten.

YEAR	TEAM	LVL	AGE	WHIP	ERA	DRA-	WARP	MPH	FB%	WHF	CSP
2018	LAD	MLB	28	1.27	3.68	119	-0.3	95.1	85.6%	27.4%	
2019	LAD	MLB	29	1.38	3.63	113	0.0	94.1	88.8%	21.4%	
2020	LAD	MLB	30	1.46	2.92	97	0.1	94.5	83.2%	23.2%	
2021 FS	LAD	MLB	31	1.38	3.85	92	0.5	94.7	85.8%	24.6%	45.5%
2021 DC	LAD	MLB	31	1.38	3.85	92	0.5	94.7	85.8%	24.6%	45.5%

Scott Alexander, continued

Pitch Shape vs LHH

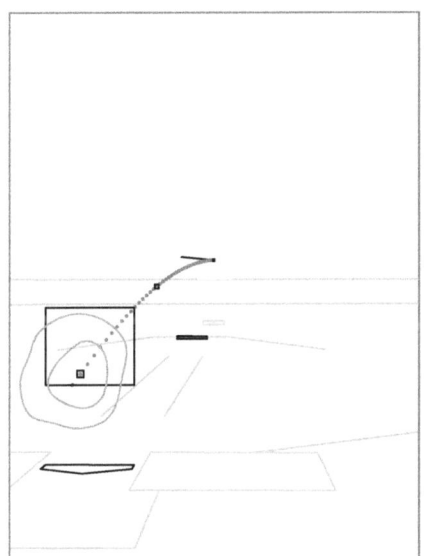

Pitch Shape vs RHH

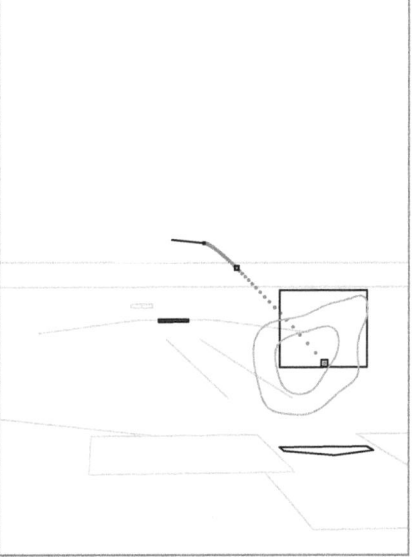

Type	Frequency	Velocity	H Movement	V Movement
☐ Sinker	81.1%	93.1 [103]	12.8 [102]	-24 [89]
▽ Slider	16.5%	87.9 [118]	-0.2 [81]	-27.5 [118]

Dodgers Player Analysis - 37

Los Angeles Dodgers 2021

Trevor Bauer RHP

Born: 01/17/91 Age: 30 Bats: R Throws: R
Height: 6'1" Weight: 205 Origin: Round 1, 2011 Draft (#3 overall)

YEAR	TEAM	LVL	AGE	W	L	SV	G	GS	IP	H	HR	BB/9	K/9	K	GB%	BABIP
2018	CLE	MLB	27	12	6	1	28	27	175^1	134	9	2.9	11.3	221	43.7%	.299
2019	CIN	MLB	28	2	5	0	10	10	56^1	57	12	3.0	10.9	68	33.5%	.321
2019	CLE	MLB	28	9	8	0	24	24	156^2	127	22	3.6	10.6	185	39.3%	.278
2020	CIN	MLB	29	5	4	0	11	11	73	41	9	2.1	12.3	100	35.4%	.215
2021 FS	LAD	MLB	30	10	7	0	26	26	150	122	23	3.2	11.7	194	38.1%	.289
2021 DC	LAD	MLB	30	11	7	0	27	27	165	134	25	3.2	11.7	214	38.1%	.289

Comparables: Jake Odorizzi, Julio Teheran, Kevin Gausman

Love him or hate him—and there are probably good reasons for both—Bauer is the most interesting player in today's game. His iconoclasm, his embrace and application of science and technology, his arrogance and his ceaseless trolling fit well in a world where nerd culture and social self-promotion are celebrated, and poorly in a game where old school stoicism has long been the example. Seeing Bauer ride the perhaps-not-that-mysterious increase in his spin rate to a Cy Young award made some feel like a lab-assisted Ivan Drago had unfairly knocked out Rocky Balboa, while others marveled that someone as human-scaled as Bauer could even compete in the ring, let alone dominate. But dominate he did, in a way that looks nothing like a fluke. Whatever your thoughts about his method or his madness, Bauer has constructed and mastered a devastating five-pitch arsenal and enters his 30s having been mostly healthy for seven straight years. That's an ace.

YEAR	TEAM	LVL	AGE	WHIP	ERA	DRA-	WARP	MPH	FB%	WHF	CSP
2018	CLE	MLB	27	1.09	2.21	55	5.7	96.5	42.2%	31.5%	
2019	CIN	MLB	28	1.35	6.39	112	0.1	96.2	45.3%	29.2%	
2019	CLE	MLB	28	1.21	3.79	96	1.9	96.7	41.2%	29.5%	
2020	CIN	MLB	29	0.79	1.73	81	1.4	96.2	47.8%	30.4%	
2021 FS	LAD	MLB	30	1.18	3.33	80	3.1	96.5	43.7%	30.1%	44.0%
2021 DC	LAD	MLB	30	1.18	3.33	80	3.4	96.5	43.7%	30.1%	44.0%

Trevor Bauer, continued

Pitch Shape vs LHH

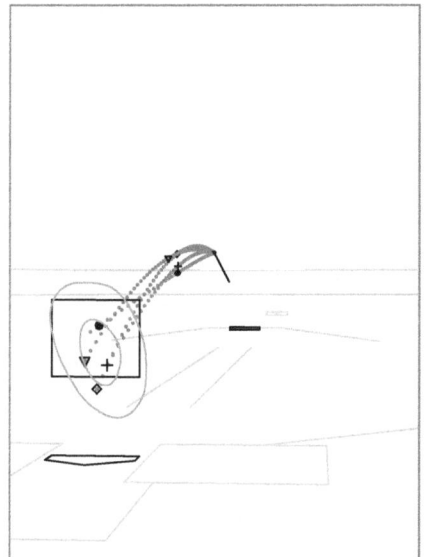

Pitch Shape vs RHH

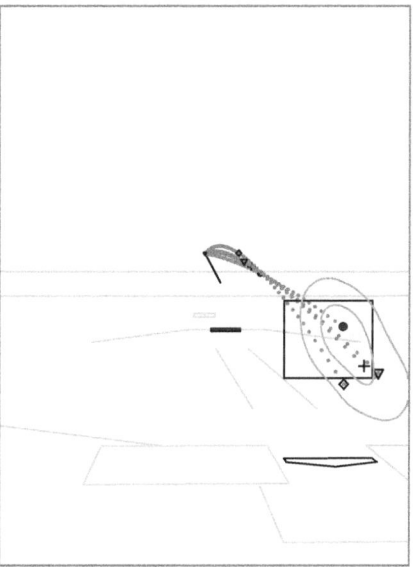

Type	Frequency	Velocity	H Movement	V Movement
● Fastball	46.5%	93.7 [104]	-8.5 [91]	-10.4 [113]
+ Cutter	19.5%	85.3 [81]	4.9 [119]	-34 [62]
▽ Slider	16.6%	80.9 [86]	15.6 [139]	-40.6 [80]
◇ Curveball	15.7%	79.9 [105]	7.9 [102]	-57.3 [80]

Walker Buehler   RHP

Born: 07/28/94 Age: 26 Bats: R Throws: R
Height: 6'2" Weight: 185 Origin: Round 1, 2015 Draft (#24 overall)

YEAR	TEAM	LVL	AGE	W	L	SV	G	GS	IP	H	HR	BB/9	K/9	K	GB%	BABIP
2018	RC	HI-A	23	0	0	0	1	1	3	2	0	3.0	15.0	5	83.3%	.333
2018	OKC	AAA	23	1	0	0	3	3	13	10	0	2.8	11.1	16	60.6%	.303
2018	LAD	MLB	23	8	5	0	24	23	137^1	95	12	2.4	9.9	151	49.6%	.249
2019	LAD	MLB	24	14	4	0	30	30	182^1	153	20	1.8	10.6	215	42.1%	.292
2020	LAD	MLB	25	1	0	0	8	8	36^2	24	7	2.7	10.3	42	36.6%	.198
2021 FS	LAD	MLB	26	10	7	0	26	26	150	125	20	2.6	10.6	175	41.9%	.285
2021 DC	LAD	MLB	26	11	7	0	27	27	156.7	131	21	2.6	10.6	183	41.9%	.285

Comparables: Luke Weaver, Luis Severino, Roberto Osuna

Blisters are a stupid part of baseball. No sour grapes here; that's just a fact. It's nice, in a sense, to know that creating extraordinary spin and speed when throwing a ball has a physical cost, but when that cost takes the form of a friction burn on a fingertip, and when that tiny injury can sideline and constrain a pitcher for weeks, it really exposes the folly and caprice of the baseball universe. Buehler has been trying to assert himself as one of the most exciting young pitchers in the majors for three years now, with a five-pitch power arsenal few can match. In 2020, though, the weakness of the skin on his index finger was enough to keep his tremendous talent from fully manifesting.

YEAR	TEAM	LVL	AGE	WHIP	ERA	DRA-	WARP	MPH	FB%	WHF	CSP
2018	RC	HI-A	23	1.00	3.00	135	0.0				
2018	OKC	AAA	23	1.08	2.08	69	0.3				
2018	LAD	MLB	23	0.96	2.62	71	3.3	98.3	59.6%	25.7%	
2019	LAD	MLB	24	1.04	3.26	59	5.7	98.4	60.2%	26.8%	
2020	LAD	MLB	25	0.95	3.44	87	0.6	99.0	62.3%	28.4%	
2021 FS	LAD	MLB	26	1.13	2.99	74	3.6	98.5	60.4%	26.9%	49.1%
2021 DC	LAD	MLB	26	1.13	2.99	74	3.8	98.5	60.4%	26.9%	49.1%

Walker Buehler, continued

Pitch Shape vs LHH

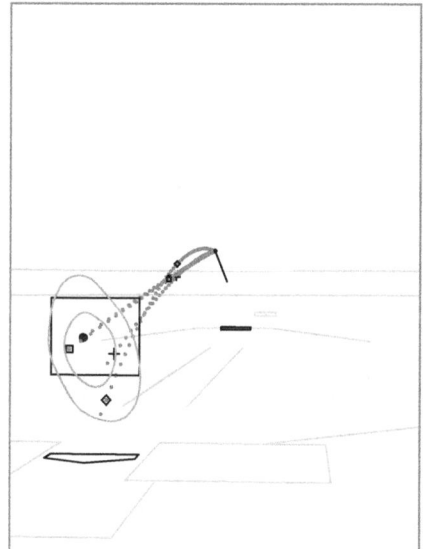

Pitch Shape vs RHH

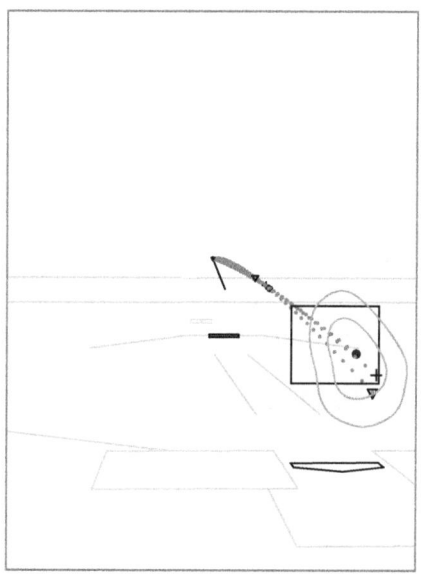

Type	Frequency	Velocity	H Movement	V Movement
● Fastball	53.7%	96.8 [113]	-4.6 [110]	-9 [118]
□ Sinker	8.7%	97.2 [124]	-12.3 [106]	-12.8 [125]
+ Cutter	14.5%	92.6 [127]	4.9 [120]	-19.1 [120]
▽ Slider	9.2%	86.5 [111]	11.1 [122]	-34.1 [99]
◇ Curveball	14.0%	81.7 [112]	10.2 [111]	-50.9 [94]

Los Angeles Dodgers 2021

Caleb Ferguson LHP
Born: 07/02/96   Age: 25   Bats: R   Throws: L
Height: 6'3"   Weight: 226   Origin: Round 38, 2014 Draft (#1149 overall)

YEAR	TEAM	LVL	AGE	W	L	SV	G	GS	IP	H	HR	BB/9	K/9	K	GB%	BABIP
2018	TUL	AA	21	3	0	0	8	8	39	31	2	2.3	9.2	40	39.8%	.284
2018	OKC	AAA	21	0	0	0	2	2	8	6	0	7.9	13.5	12	21.1%	.316
2018	LAD	MLB	21	7	2	2	29	3	49	43	8	2.2	10.8	59	45.3%	.292
2019	OKC	AAA	22	0	0	1	13	1	15[1]	9	1	2.9	15.8	27	46.2%	.320
2019	LAD	MLB	22	1	2	0	46	2	44[2]	39	7	5.4	10.9	54	38.5%	.294
2020	LAD	MLB	23	2	1	0	21	1	18[2]	16	4	1.4	13.0	27	51.1%	.293
2021 FS	LAD	MLB	24	2	2	0	57	0	50	40	6	3.6	11.1	61	43.1%	.288

Comparables: Julio Urías, Nick Neidert, Génesis Cabrera

Substituting a slider (he calls it a cutter, reinforcing the need to throw it hard) for his big-breaking curveball turned Ferguson into an elite reliever; Tommy John surgery turned him into a non-factor for 2021.

YEAR	TEAM	LVL	AGE	WHIP	ERA	DRA-	WARP	MPH	FB%	WHF	CSP
2018	TUL	AA	21	1.05	1.38	82	0.6				
2018	OKC	AAA	21	1.62	2.25	92	0.1				
2018	LAD	MLB	21	1.12	3.49	70	1.0	96.0	71.9%	26.3%	
2019	OKC	AAA	22	0.91	1.76	26	0.7				
2019	LAD	MLB	22	1.48	4.84	100	0.2	96.3	78.0%	23.4%	
2020	LAD	MLB	23	1.02	2.89	69	0.5	96.7	79.6%	29.1%	
2021 FS	LAD	MLB	24	1.21	3.16	77	0.9	96.3	76.9%	25.6%	51.1%

Caleb Ferguson, continued

Pitch Shape vs LHH

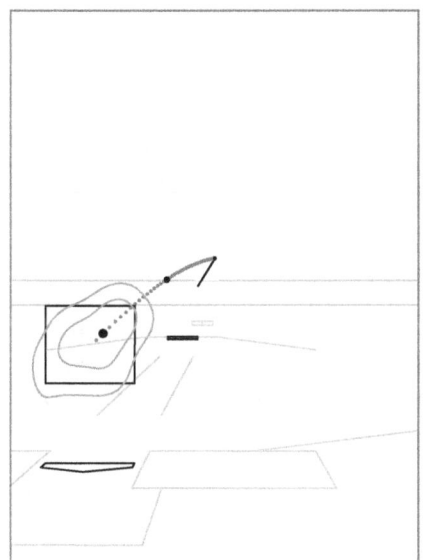

Pitch Shape vs RHH

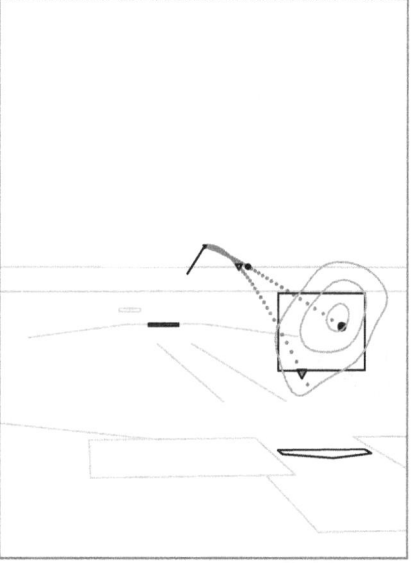

Type	Frequency	Velocity	H Movement	V Movement
● Fastball	79.6%	95.4 [109]	8.6 [91]	-12 [109]
▽ Slider	20.4%	86.5 [112]	-4.2 [96]	-33.5 [101]

Tony Gonsolin RHP

Born: 05/14/94 Age: 27 Bats: R Throws: R
Height: 6'3" Weight: 205 Origin: Round 9, 2016 Draft (#281 overall)

YEAR	TEAM	LVL	AGE	W	L	SV	G	GS	IP	H	HR	BB/9	K/9	K	GB%	BABIP
2018	RC	HI-A	24	4	2	0	17	17	83²	72	5	2.8	11.4	106	37.2%	.321
2018	TUL	AA	24	6	0	0	9	9	44¹	32	3	3.2	9.9	49	36.0%	.269
2019	OKC	AAA	25	2	4	0	13	13	41¹	41	4	4.6	10.9	50	35.0%	.327
2019	LAD	MLB	25	4	2	1	11	6	40	26	4	3.4	8.3	37	40.9%	.208
2020	LAD	MLB	26	2	2	0	9	8	46²	32	2	1.4	8.9	46	33.6%	.252
2021 FS	LAD	MLB	27	10	7	0	26	26	150	130	24	3.2	9.4	156	36.8%	.275
2021 DC	LAD	MLB	27	9	6	0	43	14	113	98	18	3.2	9.4	118	36.8%	.275

Comparables: Joe Musgrove, Kevin Gausman, Ricky Nolasco

    Pairing command with control has, perhaps, led us to think of the skill too much as a matter of location. Gonsolin poses an argument in favor of shifting that paradigm. Scouts' hesitations about him centered on his iffy command (and control), but in 2020, he shook off that criticism. A slight quieting-down of what is still a deceptive delivery, featuring a high front side and high arm slot, led to a walk rate of four percent but, more importantly, he executed consistently and missed more bats. He was first untrusted, then untrustworthy in October, but Gonsolin has all the makings of a solid three-pitch starter with good command—even if not in the traditional sense.

YEAR	TEAM	LVL	AGE	WHIP	ERA	DRA-	WARP	MPH	FB%	WHF	CSP
2018	RC	HI-A	24	1.17	2.69	80	1.3				
2018	TUL	AA	24	1.08	2.44	70	1.0				
2019	OKC	AAA	25	1.50	4.35	61	1.5				
2019	LAD	MLB	25	1.02	2.92	86	0.6	95.5	48.3%	26.9%	
2020	LAD	MLB	26	0.84	2.31	83	0.8	96.6	47.5%	29.8%	
2021 FS	LAD	MLB	27	1.22	3.59	86	2.6	96.1	47.8%	28.6%	45.0%
2021 DC	LAD	MLB	27	1.22	3.59	86	1.8	96.1	47.8%	28.6%	45.0%

Tony Gonsolin, *continued*

Pitch Shape vs LHH

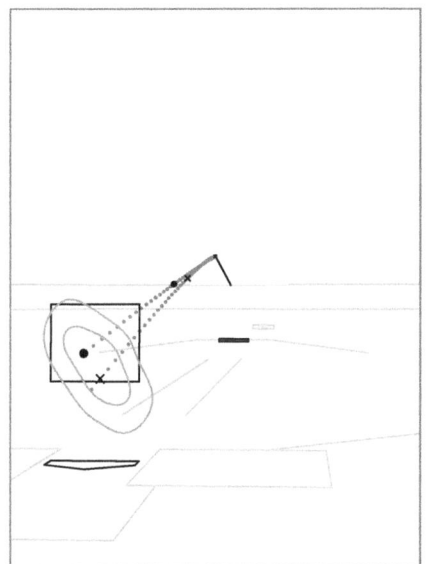

Pitch Shape vs RHH

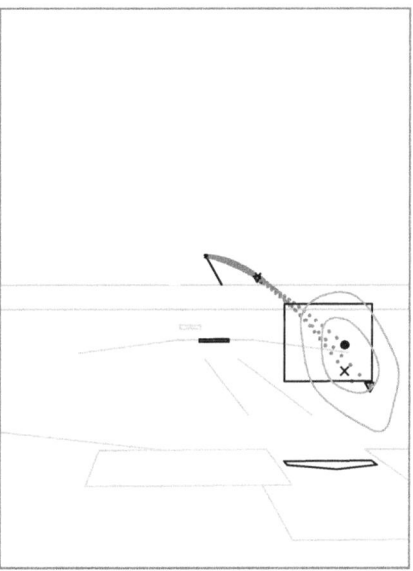

Type	Frequency	Velocity	H Movement	V Movement
● Fastball	47.5%	95.1 [108]	-8.4 [92]	-11 [112]
✕ Splitter	29.8%	85.1 [99]	-13.3 [80]	-26.6 [109]
▽ Slider	16.7%	87.4 [116]	3.6 [94]	-30.1 [111]
◇ Curveball	6.0%	81.7 [112]	4 [86]	-49.3 [98]

Los Angeles Dodgers 2021

Victor González   LHP

Born: 11/16/95   Age: 25   Bats: L   Throws: L
Height: 6'0"   Weight: 180   Origin: International Free Agent, 2012

YEAR	TEAM	LVL	AGE	W	L	SV	G	GS	IP	H	HR	BB/9	K/9	K	GB%	BABIP
2018	OGD	ROK	22	1	2	0	4	2	8	18	1	4.5	7.9	7	54.3%	.500
2018	GL	LO-A	22	0	3	0	6	6	25²	33	3	1.8	6.3	18	33.0%	.353
2019	RC	HI-A	23	2	1	0	8	5	27¹	17	0	4.6	11.9	36	47.7%	.274
2019	TUL	AA	23	3	1	2	15	8	48¹	48	4	2.6	8.2	44	52.1%	.319
2019	OKC	AAA	23	0	0	0	15	0	14	16	3	2.6	8.4	13	54.5%	.317
2020	LAD	MLB	24	3	0	0	15	1	20¹	13	0	0.9	10.2	23	69.2%	.250
2021 FS	LAD	MLB	25	2	2	0	57	0	50	46	6	3.7	8.6	47	54.0%	.290
2021 DC	LAD	MLB	25	2	2	0	44	0	49.7	46	6	3.7	8.6	47	54.0%	.290

Comparables: Max Fried, Drew Anderson, Randy Rosario

For most of his pro career, González lacked the command required of a quality big-leaguer. He had the funky, low arm slot, the wiggle on the sinker, and a decent slider, but his delivery left him spinning off toward the third-base dugout, causing insufficient precision. During the coronal interregnum, though, he made a significant mechanical change and the Dodgers found a dominant southpaw for their bullpen. By getting much deeper into his legs, González was able to maintain better posture, a more direct line to the plate and more consistent timing. The result was a run of 107 batters faced (including some key postseason appearances) with six walks, no homers allowed and all the makings of a star reliever being born.

YEAR	TEAM	LVL	AGE	WHIP	ERA	DRA-	WARP	MPH	FB%	WHF	CSP
2018	OGD	ROK	22	2.75	13.50						
2018	GL	LO-A	22	1.48	5.61	77	0.5				
2019	RC	HI-A	23	1.13	1.65	60	0.6				
2019	TUL	AA	23	1.28	2.23	94	0.2				
2019	OKC	AAA	23	1.43	3.86	99	0.2				
2020	LAD	MLB	24	0.74	1.33	64	0.6	96.4	62.8%	33.6%	
2021 FS	LAD	MLB	25	1.34	3.90	92	0.5	96.4	62.8%	33.6%	44.6%
2021 DC	LAD	MLB	25	1.34	3.90	92	0.5	96.4	62.8%	33.6%	44.6%

Victor González, continued

Pitch Shape vs LHH

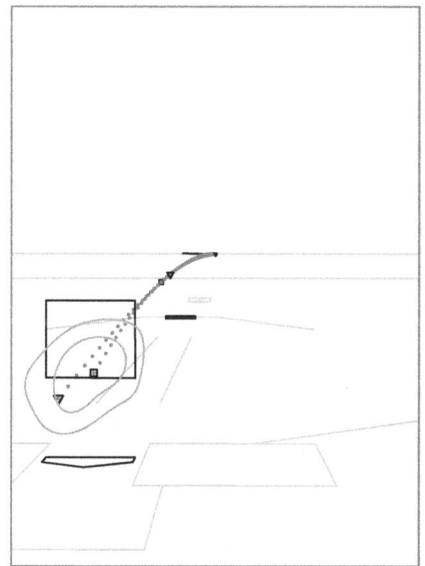

Pitch Shape vs RHH

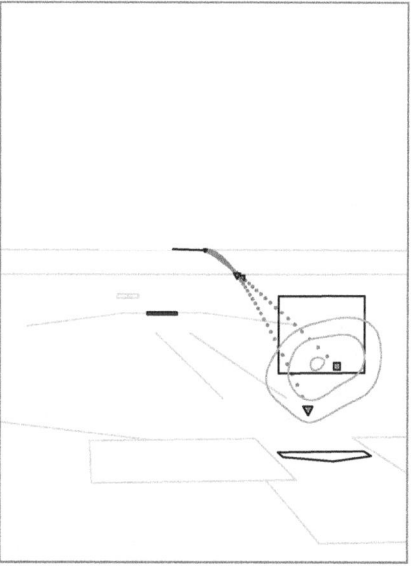

Type	Frequency	Velocity	H Movement	V Movement
● Fastball	4.1%	95.1 [108]	13.2 [69]	-17.4 [94]
□ Sinker	58.6%	94.9 [113]	16.1 [78]	-21.9 [96]
▽ Slider	35.9%	84.4 [102]	-2.7 [90]	-34.6 [97]

Brusdar Graterol RHP

Born: 08/26/98 Age: 22 Bats: R Throws: R
Height: 6'1" Weight: 265 Origin: International Free Agent, 2014

YEAR	TEAM	LVL	AGE	W	L	SV	G	GS	IP	H	HR	BB/9	K/9	K	GB%	BABIP
2018	CR	LO-A	19	3	2	0	8	8	41^1	30	3	2.0	11.1	51	64.1%	.270
2018	FTM	HI-A	19	5	2	0	11	11	60^2	59	0	2.8	8.3	56	48.3%	.343
2019	TWI	ROK	20	0	0	0	2	2	3	1	0	0.0	12.0	4	60.0%	.200
2019	PNS	AA	20	6	0	1	12	9	52^2	32	2	3.6	8.5	50	55.0%	.234
2019	ROC	AAA	20	1	0	0	4	0	5^1	4	1	3.4	11.8	7	50.0%	.273
2019	MIN	MLB	20	1	1	0	10	0	9^2	10	1	1.9	9.3	10	51.9%	.346
2020	LAD	MLB	21	1	2	0	23	2	23^1	18	1	1.2	5.0	13	63.8%	.250
2021 FS	LAD	MLB	22	2	2	4	57	0	50	47	5	3.5	8.1	44	53.9%	.294
2021 DC	LAD	MLB	22	2	2	4	49	0	49.7	47	5	3.5	8.1	44	53.9%	.294

Comparables: Bryse Wilson, Alex Reyes, Deivi García

When Graterol suffered a minor knee injury on September 10, Dave Roberts dismissed the problem by saying, "[Graterol] is a big, strong guy. He loves mangoes. I'll get him a mango and he'll be fine." That's a very common form of baseball joke. Clubhouses can be as awkward as any other workplace. People find out one thing you like or dislike, immediately stop learning about you and assume that single preference reliably defines your entire personality. As Graterol proved in the postseason, his gregariousness and competitiveness run deeper than his willingness to pitch through pain in exchange for tropical fruit. His 100 mph sinker does seem as heavy as a mango, though, and his slider is good enough to keep hitters honest. In order to make the leap to relief ace status, he'll need to develop more depth on his breaking ball.

YEAR	TEAM	LVL	AGE	WHIP	ERA	DRA-	WARP	MPH	FB%	WHF	CSP
2018	CR	LO-A	19	0.94	2.18	76	0.8				
2018	FTM	HI-A	19	1.29	3.12	88	0.7				
2019	TWI	ROK	20	0.33	0.00						
2019	PNS	AA	20	1.01	1.71	60	1.3				
2019	ROC	AAA	20	1.12	5.06	66	0.2				
2019	MIN	MLB	20	1.24	4.66	70	0.2	100.3	67.4%	18.7%	
2020	LAD	MLB	21	0.90	3.09	87	0.4	100.7	70.8%	15.2%	
2021 FS	LAD	MLB	22	1.35	4.05	94	0.4	100.6	69.9%	16.0%	54.3%
2021 DC	LAD	MLB	22	1.35	4.05	94	0.4	100.6	69.9%	16.0%	54.3%

Brusdar Graterol, continued

Pitch Shape vs LHH

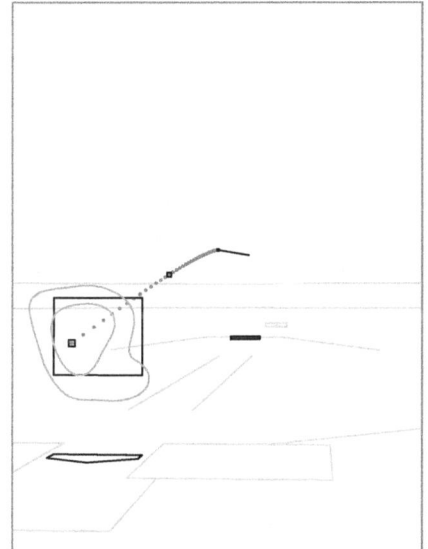

Pitch Shape vs RHH

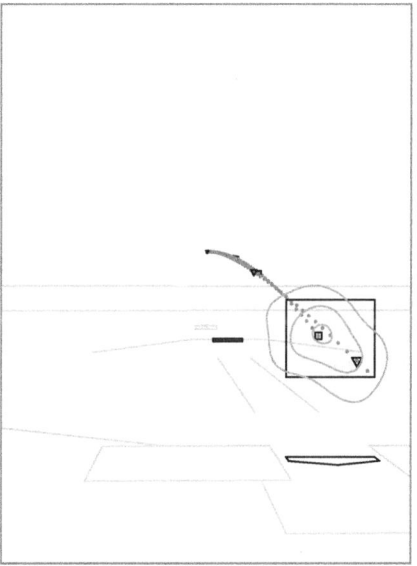

Type	Frequency	Velocity	H Movement	V Movement
● Fastball	3.4%	98.9 [120]	-7.9 [94]	-12.5 [108]
☐ Sinker	67.4%	99.3 [135]	-12.8 [102]	-17.6 [110]
▽ Slider	28.9%	89.1 [123]	6.5 [105]	-26.1 [122]

Kenley Jansen RHP

Born: 09/30/87 Age: 33 Bats: S Throws: R
Height: 6'5" Weight: 265 Origin: International Free Agent, 2004

YEAR	TEAM	LVL	AGE	W	L	SV	G	GS	IP	H	HR	BB/9	K/9	K	GB%	BABIP
2018	LAD	MLB	30	1	5	38	69	0	71²	54	13	2.1	10.3	82	35.6%	.234
2019	LAD	MLB	31	5	3	33	62	0	63	51	9	2.3	11.4	80	32.5%	.273
2020	LAD	MLB	32	3	1	11	27	0	24¹	19	2	3.3	12.2	33	24.6%	.309
2021 FS	LAD	MLB	33	3	2	37	57	0	50	38	6	2.0	10.9	60	33.4%	.273
2021 DC	LAD	MLB	33	2	1	37	44	0	49.7	38	6	2.0	10.9	60	33.4%	.273

Comparables: Craig Kimbrel, Dellin Betances, Francisco Rodríguez

Dave Roberts has a special relationship with his future Hall of Fame closer. He treats Jansen like a beloved son, giving him countless opportunities to be the hero and trusting him more than anyone else might. Because of that foundation of love and respect, he also earned the right to challenge Jansen and he did so in 2020. Roberts noted that Jansen's velocity would sometimes lag in a given appearance, unless or until he got into trouble. He instructed the aging relief ace, in so many words, not to keep any of his best stuff in the tank. When Jansen's movement and command failed him late in the season, Roberts (tactfully, but decisively) let Julio Urías seal the club's pennant and World Series title. To Jansen's credit, he was much more glad to have won than indignant at being passed over. He's likely finished as an elite closer, but far from finished as a solid reliever and teammate.

YEAR	TEAM	LVL	AGE	WHIP	ERA	DRA-	WARP	MPH	FB%	WHF	CSP
2018	LAD	MLB	30	0.99	3.01	57	2.0	94.7	94.2%	28.2%	
2019	LAD	MLB	31	1.06	3.71	72	1.3	94.3	87.7%	32.2%	
2020	LAD	MLB	32	1.15	3.33	82	0.4	93.7	90.4%	30.8%	
2021 FS	LAD	MLB	33	1.00	2.37	62	1.3	94.2	90.1%	30.8%	47.4%
2021 DC	LAD	MLB	33	1.00	2.37	62	1.3	94.2	90.1%	30.8%	47.4%

Kenley Jansen, continued

Pitch Shape vs LHH	Pitch Shape vs RHH
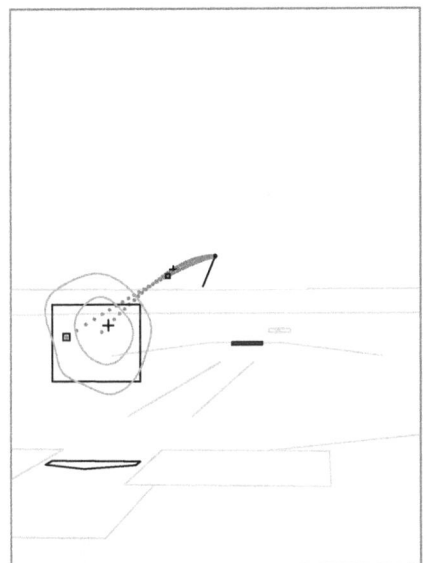	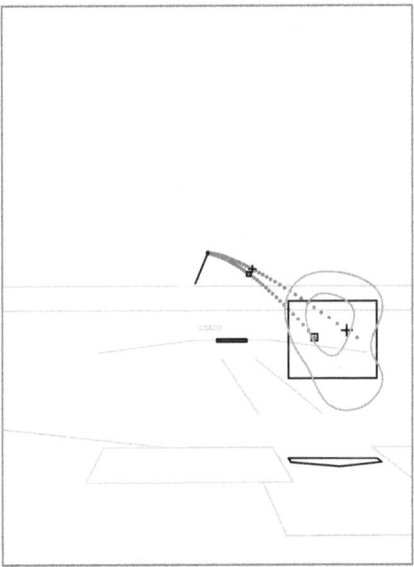

Type	Frequency	Velocity	H Movement	V Movement
☐ Sinker	28.3%	92.3 [99]	-6.2 [150]	-12.7 [125]
+ Cutter	62.1%	90.9 [116]	7.2 [134]	-17.6 [126]
▽ Slider	9.6%	81.6 [89]	6.3 [104]	-40.7 [80]

Joe Kelly RHP

Born: 06/09/88 Age: 33 Bats: R Throws: R
Height: 6'1" Weight: 174 Origin: Round 3, 2009 Draft (#98 overall)

YEAR	TEAM	LVL	AGE	W	L	SV	G	GS	IP	H	HR	BB/9	K/9	K	GB%	BABIP
2018	BOS	MLB	30	4	2	2	73	0	65^2	57	4	4.4	9.3	68	48.3%	.301
2019	LAD	MLB	31	5	4	1	55	0	51^1	49	6	3.9	10.9	62	62.6%	.323
2020	LAD	MLB	32	0	0	0	12	1	10	8	0	6.3	8.1	9	57.7%	.308
2021 FS	LAD	MLB	33	2	2	0	57	0	50	45	7	4.3	9.5	52	51.7%	.290
2021 DC	LAD	MLB	33	1	1	0	38	0	49.7	45	7	4.3	9.5	52	51.7%	.290

Comparables: Trevor Cahill, Diego Segui, Jhoulys Chacín

When life throws you curveballs, throw them back. Or at some Astros. Kelly certainly did. After (ahem) unsuccessful attempts to improve his control during quarantine, he simply showed up and started spinning his vicious power curve—the one that sometimes eclipses 90 miles per hour, with genuine curveball depth. No pitcher in the PITCHf/x Era has thrown curves as often as Kelly did in 2020. It didn't turn him into an unstoppable force because he still struggles to stay healthy and to throw strikes, but it makes him a bit more interesting and (as Kelly does so well) it keeps one wondering: what if his simplified arsenal and breaking-ball primacy finally allow him to tap into his full potential?

YEAR	TEAM	LVL	AGE	WHIP	ERA	DRA-	WARP	MPH	FB%	WHF	CSP
2018	BOS	MLB	30	1.36	4.39	101	0.3	100.2	55.4%	25.7%	
2019	LAD	MLB	31	1.38	4.56	67	1.2	99.6	50.9%	26.4%	
2020	LAD	MLB	32	1.50	1.80	86	0.2	98.2	36.8%	27.5%	
2021 FS	LAD	MLB	33	1.39	4.16	96	0.3	99.6	50.3%	26.3%	47.0%
2021 DC	LAD	MLB	33	1.39	4.16	96	0.3	99.6	50.3%	26.3%	47.0%

Joe Kelly, continued

Pitch Shape vs LHH

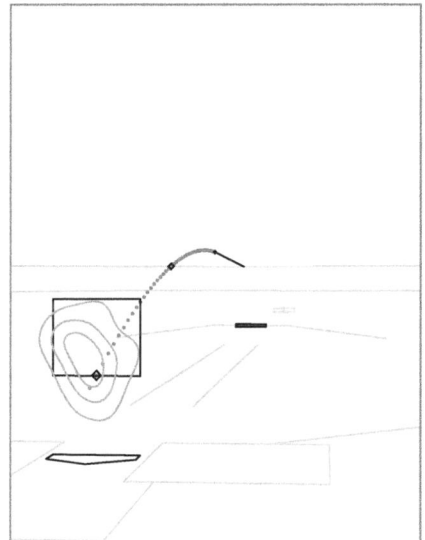

Pitch Shape vs RHH

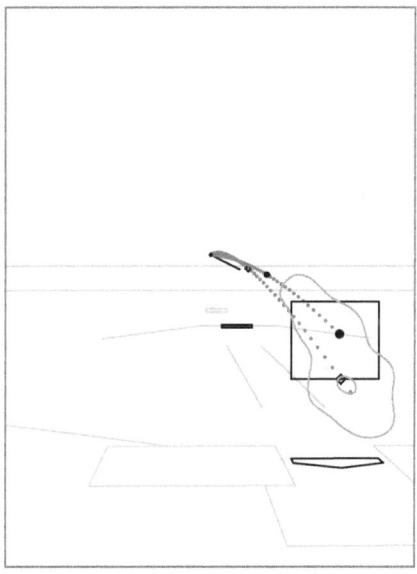

Type	Frequency	Velocity	H Movement	V Movement
● Fastball	21.6%	97.3 [115]	-10.6 [81]	-14.7 [101]
□ Sinker	15.2%	96.4 [121]	-14.1 [92]	-19.8 [102]
◇ Curveball	63.2%	87.1 [133]	9 [106]	-41.6 [115]

Clayton Kershaw LHP

Born: 03/19/88   Age: 33   Bats: L   Throws: L
Height: 6'4"   Weight: 225   Origin: Round 1, 2006 Draft (#7 overall)

YEAR	TEAM	LVL	AGE	W	L	SV	G	GS	IP	H	HR	BB/9	K/9	K	GB%	BABIP
2018	LAD	MLB	30	9	5	0	26	26	161[1]	139	17	1.6	8.6	155	47.7%	.276
2019	LAD	MLB	31	16	5	0	29	28	178[1]	145	28	2.1	9.5	189	46.3%	.267
2020	LAD	MLB	32	6	2	0	10	10	58[1]	41	8	1.2	9.6	62	52.7%	.232
2021 FS	LAD	MLB	33	10	6	0	26	26	150	126	17	1.8	9.6	160	49.6%	.282
2021 DC	LAD	MLB	33	12	6	0	27	27	167.7	141	19	1.8	9.6	180	49.6%	.282

Comparables: Felix Hernandez, Jacob deGrom, Carlos Carrasco

When the Dodgers developed an official (non-exclusive) partnership with Driveline Baseball, they surely envisioned something like Kershaw's 2020. Folding the resources that organization offers into the structure of the team's instruction and development makes it safer and easier for a future Hall of Famer to make what might otherwise feel like a desperate move. Besides, when attaching the term 'Driveline' to pitching, it's just Kershaw's style of hitch-and-fire, over-the-top, straight-ahead mechanics that spring to mind. Through his work at Driveline and elsewhere, the best southpaw of his generation added back some lost velocity, rediscovered the vertical separation he wanted on his slider and reclaimed his ace status in the Dodgers rotation—if only for one more year.

YEAR	TEAM	LVL	AGE	WHIP	ERA	DRA-	WARP	MPH	FB%	WHF	CSP
2018	LAD	MLB	30	1.04	2.73	69	4.1	92.5	41.2%	23.0%	
2019	LAD	MLB	31	1.04	3.03	68	4.7	91.7	43.9%	28.1%	
2020	LAD	MLB	32	0.84	2.16	75	1.3	93.0	40.8%	27.7%	
2021 FS	LAD	MLB	33	1.04	2.39	64	4.5	92.2	42.5%	26.8%	48.5%
2021 DC	LAD	MLB	33	1.04	2.39	64	5.0	92.2	42.5%	26.8%	48.5%

Clayton Kershaw, continued

Pitch Shape vs LHH

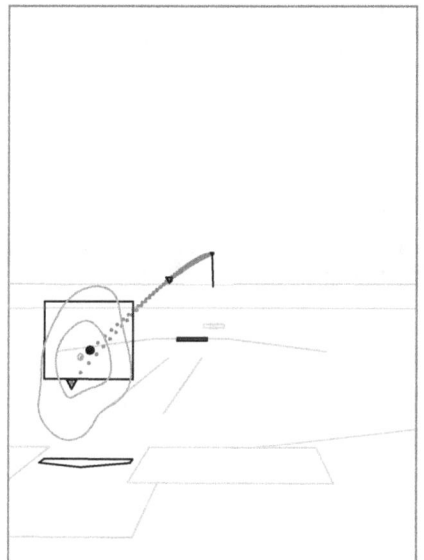

Pitch Shape vs RHH

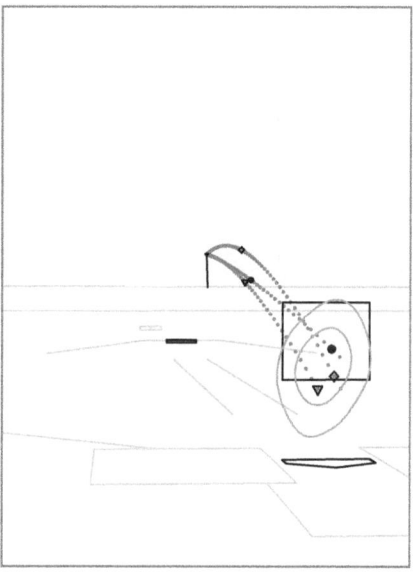

Type	Frequency	Velocity	H Movement	V Movement
● Fastball	40.8%	91.6 [97]	-0.4 [134]	-11.9 [109]
▽ Slider	40.2%	87.9 [118]	-4.1 [96]	-24.6 [127]
◇ Curveball	18.8%	74.2 [83]	-3.9 [85]	-59.3 [76]

Los Angeles Dodgers 2021

Corey Knebel   RHP
Born: 11/26/91   Age: 29   Bats: R   Throws: R
Height: 6'3"   Weight: 224   Origin: Round 1, 2013 Draft (#39 overall)

YEAR	TEAM	LVL	AGE	W	L	SV	G	GS	IP	H	HR	BB/9	K/9	K	GB%	BABIP
2018	MIL	MLB	26	4	3	16	57	0	55^1	38	7	3.6	14.3	88	49.5%	.304
2020	MIL	MLB	28	0	0	0	15	0	13^1	15	4	5.4	10.1	15	33.3%	.314
2021 FS	LAD	MLB	29	2	2	0	57	0	50	39	6	4.5	11.6	64	41.0%	.285
2021 DC	LAD	MLB	29	1	1	0	38	0	44	34	6	4.5	11.6	57	41.0%	.285

Comparables: Dominic Leone, Cam Bedrosian, Carl Edwards Jr.

He still spins his fastball and knuckle-curve well, but Knebel didn't bring his full velocity back from Tommy John surgery, and hitters noticed.

YEAR	TEAM	LVL	AGE	WHIP	ERA	DRA-	WARP	MPH	FB%	WHF	CSP
2018	MIL	MLB	26	1.08	3.58	56	1.5	98.5	70.9%	32.3%	
2020	MIL	MLB	28	1.73	6.08	121	0.0	96.4	62.7%	21.8%	
2021 FS	LAD	MLB	29	1.29	3.53	84	0.7	97.6	67.3%	27.6%	47.1%
2021 DC	LAD	MLB	29	1.29	3.53	84	0.6	97.6	67.3%	27.6%	47.1%

Corey Knebel, continued

Pitch Shape vs LHH

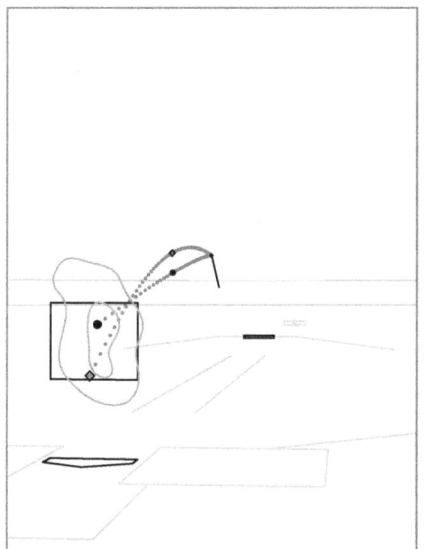

Pitch Shape vs RHH

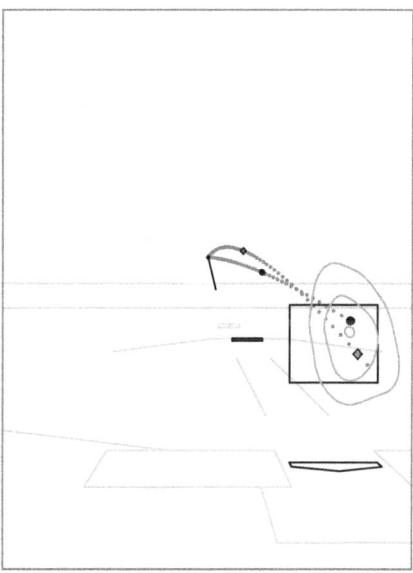

Type	Frequency	Velocity	H Movement	V Movement
● Fastball	62.7%	94.6 [106]	-3.5 [115]	-11.7 [110]
▲ Changeup	3.4%	88 [111]	-12.4 [96]	-25.8 [105]
◇ Curveball	33.8%	78.4 [99]	11.6 [116]	-55.1 [85]

Los Angeles Dodgers 2021

Dustin May RHP
Born: 09/06/97 Age: 23 Bats: R Throws: R
Height: 6'6" Weight: 180 Origin: Round 3, 2016 Draft (#101 overall)

YEAR	TEAM	LVL	AGE	W	L	SV	G	GS	IP	H	HR	BB/9	K/9	K	GB%	BABIP
2018	RC	HI-A	20	7	3	0	17	17	98^1	91	9	1.6	8.6	94	55.9%	.296
2018	TUL	AA	20	2	2	0	6	6	34^1	27	0	3.1	7.3	28	53.5%	.267
2019	TUL	AA	21	3	5	0	15	15	79^1	71	5	2.3	9.8	86	50.5%	.311
2019	OKC	AAA	21	3	0	0	5	5	27^1	21	0	3.0	7.9	24	59.2%	.280
2019	LAD	MLB	21	2	3	0	14	4	34^2	33	2	1.3	8.3	32	45.0%	.316
2020	LAD	MLB	22	3	1	0	12	10	56	45	9	2.6	7.1	44	53.4%	.235
2021 FS	LAD	MLB	23	9	8	0	26	26	150	147	20	2.8	7.9	132	50.8%	.292
2021 DC	LAD	MLB	23	8	6	0	43	14	111.7	109	15	2.8	7.9	98	50.8%	.292

Comparables: Luis Severino, Lucas Giolito, Bryse Wilson

Did you know May is from Justin, TX? That's an awfully good setup, for either a Dr. Seuss riff or an Abbott and Costello homage. This is the guy who, by loading up on protein between workouts each winter, has steadily packed good weight onto his Seussian frame, and whose competitiveness and work ethic have helped him become one of the league's hardest throwers. Despite the distinctly modern velocity, he's as much of a throwback as a Vaudeville partner act, having not only junked his four-seamer in favor of a zone-pounding, grounder-inducing sinker, but electing a slurve he feels confident throwing for strikes over the bat-missing yakker that gave him such strikeout upside. If he can make a tweak or two to get those whiffs back, oh, the places he'll go.

YEAR	TEAM	LVL	AGE	WHIP	ERA	DRA-	WARP	MPH	FB%	WHF	CSP
2018	RC	HI-A	20	1.10	3.29	88	1.1				
2018	TUL	AA	20	1.14	3.67	88	0.4				
2019	TUL	AA	21	1.15	3.74	78	1.1				
2019	OKC	AAA	21	1.10	2.30	39	1.3				
2019	LAD	MLB	21	1.10	3.63	93	0.4	98.0	88.2%	20.6%	
2020	LAD	MLB	22	1.09	2.57	91	0.8	99.5	81.5%	19.2%	
2021 FS	LAD	MLB	23	1.29	4.01	95	1.9	99.0	83.5%	19.6%	52.8%
2021 DC	LAD	MLB	23	1.29	4.01	95	1.2	99.0	83.5%	19.6%	52.8%

Dustin May, continued

Pitch Shape vs LHH

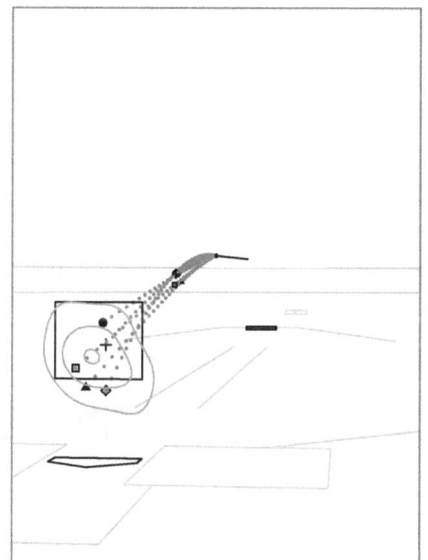

Pitch Shape vs RHH

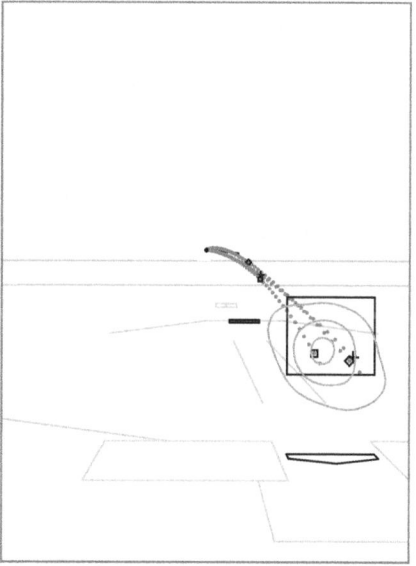

Type	Frequency	Velocity	H Movement	V Movement
● Fastball	6.5%	99 [121]	-9.7 [85]	-12.2 [109]
☐ Sinker	50.5%	97.9 [128]	-16.8 [73]	-18.9 [105]
+ Cutter	24.6%	93.6 [133]	0.2 [89]	-21.3 [111]
▲ Changeup	5.1%	90.7 [122]	-13.7 [90]	-26.5 [103]
◇ Curveball	13.4%	86.8 [132]	9.1 [106]	-37.7 [124]

Jake McGee LHP

Born: 08/06/86   Age: 34   Bats: L   Throws: L
Height: 6'4"   Weight: 229   Origin: Round 5, 2004 Draft (#135 overall)

YEAR	TEAM	LVL	AGE	W	L	SV	G	GS	IP	H	HR	BB/9	K/9	K	GB%	BABIP
2018	COL	MLB	31	2	4	1	61	0	51^1	59	10	2.8	8.2	47	40.7%	.327
2019	COL	MLB	32	0	2	0	45	0	41^1	47	11	2.4	7.6	35	35.1%	.300
2020	LAD	MLB	33	3	1	0	24	0	20^1	14	2	1.3	14.6	33	37.2%	.300
2021 FS	LAD	MLB	34	2	2	7	57	0	50	44	7	2.6	9.5	52	38.0%	.281
2021 DC	LAD	MLB	34	3	3	7	67	0	58	51	8	2.6	9.5	61	38.0%	.281

Comparables: Nick Vincent, Chaz Roe, Oliver Drake

Small mechanical changes can sometimes beget big differences in the quality of a pitcher's stuff. In McGee's case, a slight alteration to his arm path let him reclaim the 1.5 mph he'd lost over the previous two years. As the most fastball-heavy hurler in the majors, McGee needs that extra juice more than anyone, thus it made a huge difference when he rediscovered it. He still requires limited, intelligent usage, but his utility in the right role is considerable.

YEAR	TEAM	LVL	AGE	WHIP	ERA	DRA-	WARP	MPH	FB%	WHF	CSP
2018	COL	MLB	31	1.46	6.49	137	-0.7	96.2	86.3%	22.4%	
2019	COL	MLB	32	1.40	4.35	129	-0.4	95.6	80.4%	19.5%	
2020	LAD	MLB	33	0.84	2.66	65	0.6	96.5	96.9%	33.3%	
2021 FS	LAD	MLB	34	1.18	3.44	88	0.6	96.0	87.1%	24.6%	54.4%
2021 DC	LAD	MLB	34	1.18	3.44	88	0.7	96.0	87.1%	24.6%	54.4%

Jake McGee, continued

Pitch Shape vs LHH

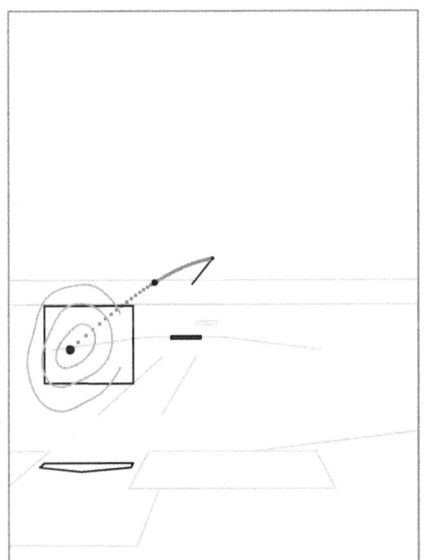

Pitch Shape vs RHH

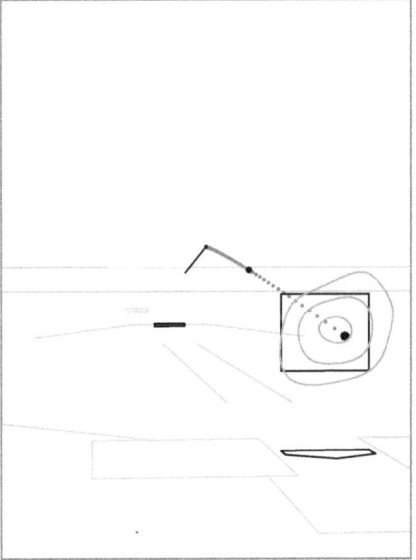

Type	Frequency	Velocity	H Movement	V Movement
● Fastball	94.9%	94.9 [107]	10.1 [83]	-13.6 [105]
▽ Slider	3.0%	82.5 [93]	-2.8 [91]	-35.5 [95]

Dennis Santana RHP

Born: 04/12/96 Age: 25 Bats: R Throws: R
Height: 6'2" Weight: 190 Origin: International Free Agent, 2013

YEAR	TEAM	LVL	AGE	W	L	SV	G	GS	IP	H	HR	BB/9	K/9	K	GB%	BABIP
2018	TUL	AA	22	0	2	0	8	8	38²	26	3	3.3	11.9	51	53.3%	.261
2018	OKC	AAA	22	1	1	0	2	2	11	10	0	1.6	11.5	14	41.4%	.357
2018	LAD	MLB	22	1	0	0	1	0	3²	6	0	2.5	9.8	4	23.1%	.500
2019	OKC	AAA	23	5	9	0	27	17	93¹	111	16	5.1	10.1	105	42.2%	.365
2019	LAD	MLB	23	0	0	0	3	0	5	6	1	7.2	10.8	6	46.7%	.357
2020	LAD	MLB	24	1	2	0	12	0	17	15	4	3.7	9.5	18	32.6%	.262
2021 FS	LAD	MLB	25	2	3	0	57	0	50	45	8	4.7	9.4	52	41.2%	.287
2021 DC	LAD	MLB	25	3	2	0	32	3	35	32	5	4.7	9.4	36	41.2%	.287

Comparables: Touki Toussaint, Zack Littell, Tyler Mahle

The highlight of Santana's season came in a late-July outing against Houston that felt like a late-September affair, as he struck out four over 2 1/3 innings—all in extras—spurring the Dodgers to a 4-2 win.

YEAR	TEAM	LVL	AGE	WHIP	ERA	DRA-	WARP	MPH	FB%	WHF	CSP
2018	TUL	AA	22	1.03	2.56	55	1.2				
2018	OKC	AAA	22	1.09	2.45	57	0.4				
2018	LAD	MLB	22	1.91	12.27	84	0.0	95.5	53.6%	31.2%	
2019	OKC	AAA	23	1.76	6.94	133	0.1				
2019	LAD	MLB	23	2.00	7.20	107	0.0	94.5	56.7%	30.4%	
2020	LAD	MLB	24	1.29	5.29	111	0.1	96.3	38.7%	28.3%	
2021 FS	LAD	MLB	25	1.44	4.72	105	0.1	95.9	43.0%	28.9%	48.3%
2021 DC	LAD	MLB	25	1.44	4.72	105	0.1	95.9	43.0%	28.9%	48.3%

Dennis Santana, continued

Pitch Shape vs LHH
Pitch Shape vs RHH

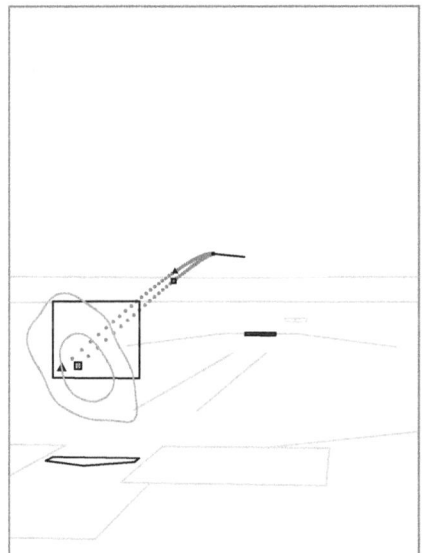
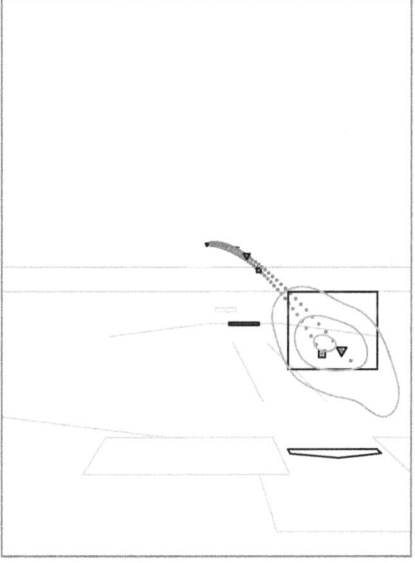

Type	Frequency	Velocity	H Movement	V Movement
● Fastball	4.6%	95.4 [109]	-11.4 [78]	-13.9 [104]
□ Sinker	34.2%	94.3 [110]	-15.6 [81]	-21 [98]
▲ Changeup	15.1%	86.7 [106]	-14 [88]	-27 [101]
▽ Slider	46.1%	84.3 [102]	4.3 [96]	-35.9 [94]

Blake Treinen RHP

Born: 06/30/88 Age: 33 Bats: R Throws: R
Height: 6'5" Weight: 225 Origin: Round 7, 2011 Draft (#226 overall)

YEAR	TEAM	LVL	AGE	W	L	SV	G	GS	IP	H	HR	BB/9	K/9	K	GB%	BABIP
2018	OAK	MLB	30	9	2	38	68	0	80^1	46	2	2.4	11.2	100	51.0%	.233
2019	OAK	MLB	31	6	5	16	57	0	58^2	58	9	5.7	9.1	59	43.2%	.308
2020	LAD	MLB	32	3	3	1	27	0	25^2	23	1	2.8	7.7	22	65.3%	.297
2021 FS	LAD	MLB	33	2	2	7	57	0	50	45	5	3.9	8.9	49	54.1%	.294
2021 DC	LAD	MLB	33	2	2	7	44	0	49.7	45	5	3.9	8.9	49	54.1%	.294

Comparables: Pedro Báez, Steve Cishek, Hector Rondón

The 2018 version of Treinen, with the extraordinary ability to both limit hard contact and miss bats at elite rates, was a two-fastball guy. He also added a cutter that year, as a variant on his slider. With four pitches, he was able to neutralize left-handed batters for the first time, elevating him to relief ace status. Alas, that proved too hard a balance to sustain—at least at that level. After he crashed back to Earth, he landed with the Dodgers, a one-fastball organization who had him put the four-seamer and cutter on the shelf against righties and minimized his exposure to lefties. Now he's a fireballing sinker-slider monster against righties, with the consistent execution and confidence to use his weaker offerings to keep southpaws off balance. The 2018 version of him is gone for good, but so is the 2018 version of you, dear reader.

YEAR	TEAM	LVL	AGE	WHIP	ERA	DRA-	WARP	MPH	FB%	WHF	CSP
2018	OAK	MLB	30	0.83	0.78	49	2.5	99.3	67.1%	35.8%	
2019	OAK	MLB	31	1.62	4.91	115	-0.2	98.5	67.1%	26.1%	
2020	LAD	MLB	32	1.21	3.86	76	0.6	98.3	64.9%	22.9%	
2021 FS	LAD	MLB	33	1.35	3.72	89	0.5	98.6	66.5%	27.8%	45.4%
2021 DC	LAD	MLB	33	1.35	3.72	89	0.5	98.6	66.5%	27.8%	45.4%

Blake Treinen, continued

Pitch Shape vs LHH	Pitch Shape vs RHH
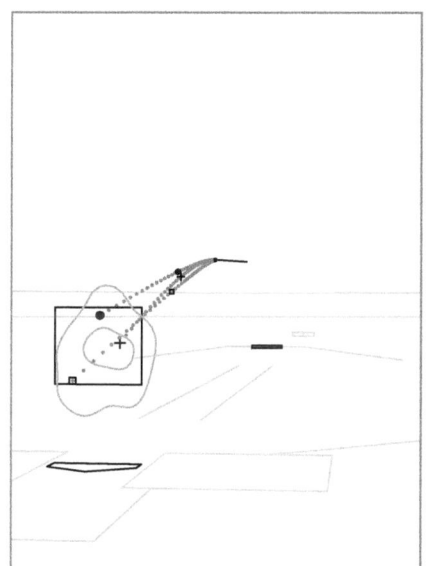	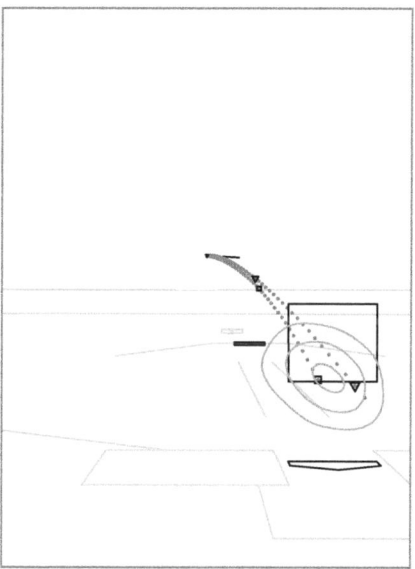

Type	Frequency	Velocity	H Movement	V Movement
● Fastball	8.0%	97.1 [114]	-9.4 [87]	-13.7 [104]
☐ Sinker	56.3%	96.9 [123]	-15.8 [80]	-20.6 [100]
+ Cutter	8.8%	94.2 [137]	0.4 [90]	-19.8 [117]
▽ Slider	26.0%	88.4 [120]	3.1 [92]	-33.8 [100]

Julio Urías LHP

Born: 08/12/96 Age: 24 Bats: L Throws: L
Height: 6'0" Weight: 225 Origin: International Free Agent, 2012

YEAR	TEAM	LVL	AGE	W	L	SV	G	GS	IP	H	HR	BB/9	K/9	K	GB%	BABIP
2018	RC	HI-A	21	0	0	0	4	4	7^1	6	3	4.9	16.0	13	46.2%	.300
2018	LAD	MLB	21	0	0	0	3	0	4	1	0	0.0	15.8	7	50.0%	.167
2019	LAD	MLB	22	4	3	4	37	8	79^2	59	7	3.1	9.6	85	38.8%	.257
2020	LAD	MLB	23	3	0	0	11	10	55	45	5	2.9	7.4	45	32.3%	.256
2021 FS	LAD	MLB	24	9	8	0	26	26	150	135	21	3.7	8.8	147	36.5%	.281
2021 DC	LAD	MLB	24	8	7	0	39	19	113.7	102	16	3.7	8.8	111	36.5%	.281

Comparables: Taijuan Walker, Junior Fernández, Sandy Alcantara

    One can tell the story of Urías' 2020 in many ways. There's a sonorous historical echo here, as one lightly scouted left-hander from western Mexico stepped forward to take on a dominant role for the Dodgers in October. Even his delivery occasionally evoked Fernando Valenzuela. The former phenom also made huge, profoundly modern developmental strides, adding depth to his changeup, lateral movement to both of his breaking balls and (at long last, at the urging of Dave Roberts and Mark Prior) the consistent zone-pounding approach that had been missing in the past. Still, it feels important to sum things up this way, too: After four years of trepidation over whether Aroldis Chapman or Roberto Osuna would record the final out of a World Series, a known perpetrator of domestic violence actually did so. By most accounts, Urías has shown both contrition and thoughtful dedication to improving his behavior going forward, but he still shoved his girlfriend to the ground in a parking lot. His heroism in October doesn't erase those actions or the pain they caused—not only to his family but to victims everywhere.

YEAR	TEAM	LVL	AGE	WHIP	ERA	DRA-	WARP	MPH	FB%	WHF	CSP
2018	RC	HI-A	21	1.36	4.91	67	0.2				
2018	LAD	MLB	21	0.25	0.00	42	0.1	95.2	69.0%	39.4%	
2019	LAD	MLB	22	1.08	2.49	69	1.8	97.1	60.3%	29.9%	
2020	LAD	MLB	23	1.15	3.27	107	0.3	95.6	56.3%	26.0%	
2021 FS	LAD	MLB	24	1.31	3.82	91	2.2	96.3	58.5%	28.1%	48.9%
2021 DC	LAD	MLB	24	1.31	3.82	91	1.4	96.3	58.5%	28.1%	48.9%

Julio Urías, continued

Pitch Shape vs LHH

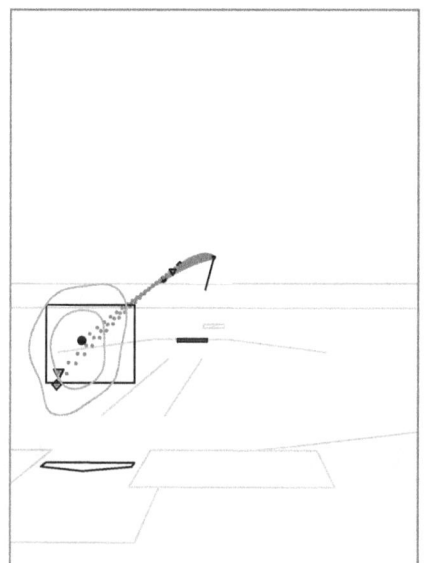

Pitch Shape vs RHH

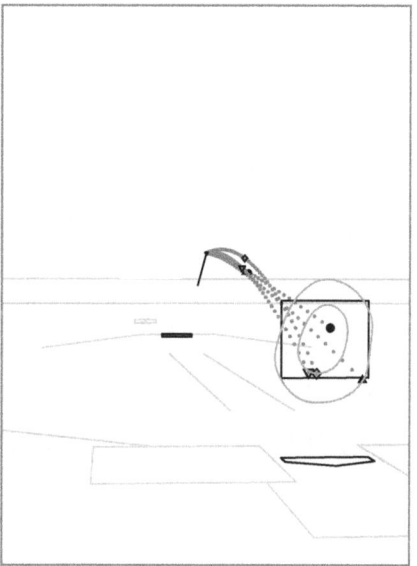

Type	Frequency	Velocity	H Movement	V Movement
● Fastball	56.0%	94.2 [105]	3.8 [114]	-12.1 [109]
▲ Changeup	13.3%	84.9 [99]	13.3 [91]	-27.4 [100]
▽ Slider	12.6%	84 [100]	-9 [114]	-32.7 [103]
◇ Curveball	17.8%	79.7 [104]	-14 [126]	-43.1 [112]

Alex Vesia   LHP

Born: 04/11/96   Age: 25   Bats: L   Throws: L
Height: 6'1"   Weight: 209   Origin: Round 17, 2018 Draft (#507 overall)

YEAR	TEAM	LVL	AGE	W	L	SV	G	GS	IP	H	HR	BB/9	K/9	K	GB%	BABIP
2018	MRL	ROK	22	1	0	0	4	0	8^2	4	0	3.1	7.3	7	52.2%	.174
2018	BAT	SS	22	3	0	0	10	0	24^2	27	1	1.5	11.3	31	31.3%	.394
2019	CLI	LO-A	23	1	2	3	19	1	31^2	24	1	4.8	14.5	51	27.3%	.359
2019	JUP	HI-A	23	4	0	1	10	0	18^2	12	2	0.5	11.6	24	43.2%	.244
2019	JAX	AA	23	2	0	1	9	0	16^1	8	0	0.6	13.8	25	41.4%	.286
2020	MIA	MLB	24	0	1	0	5	0	4^1	7	3	14.5	10.4	5	20.0%	.333
2021 FS	LAD	MLB	25	2	2	0	57	0	50	46	8	4.4	9.9	54	37.8%	.294
2021 DC	LAD	MLB	25	2	2	0	47	0	33	30	5	4.4	9.9	36	37.8%	.294

Comparables: Aaron Fletcher, Phillip Diehl, Alex Reyes

When they said the majors were going to be tough, they probably didn't mean this. Vesia started his debut season by taking the loss on the weekend that COVID-19 sidelined half of the Marlins roster and ended it by giving up five runs in a game Miami was already losing by 11.

YEAR	TEAM	LVL	AGE	WHIP	ERA	DRA-	WARP	MPH	FB%	WHF	CSP
2018	MRL	ROK	22	0.81	0.00						
2018	BAT	SS	22	1.26	1.82	191	-1.1				
2019	CLI	LO-A	23	1.29	2.56	71	0.5				
2019	JUP	HI-A	23	0.70	1.93	49	0.5				
2019	JAX	AA	23	0.55	0.00	53	0.4				
2020	MIA	MLB	24	3.23	18.69	161	-0.1	93.1	72.9%	28.3%	
2021 FS	LAD	MLB	25	1.42	4.53	104	0.1	93.1	72.9%	28.3%	46.7%
2021 DC	LAD	MLB	25	1.42	4.53	104	0.1	93.1	72.9%	28.3%	46.7%

Alex Vesia, continued

Pitch Shape vs LHH

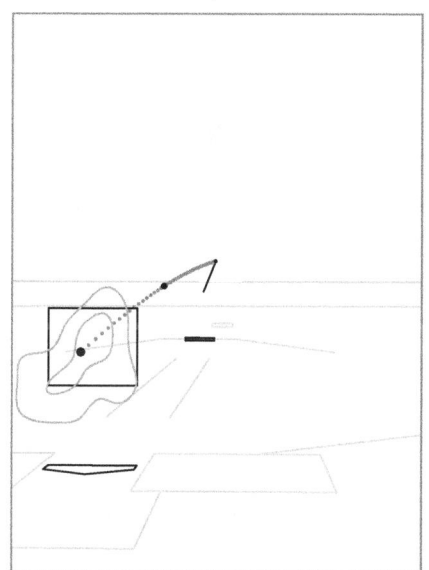

Pitch Shape vs RHH

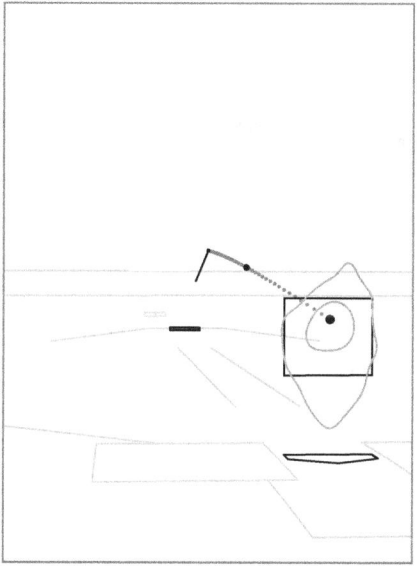

Type	Frequency	Velocity	H Movement	V Movement
● Fastball	72.9%	91.9 [98]	7.1 [98]	-11 [112]
▲ Changeup	18.0%	84.6 [98]	12.1 [98]	-24.2 [109]
▽ Slider	9.0%	84.3 [102]	-5.8 [102]	-31.2 [107]

Los Angeles Dodgers 2021

PLAYER COMMENTS WITHOUT GRAPHS

Jacob Amaya SS
Born: 09/03/98 Age: 22 Bats: R Throws: R
Height: 6'0" Weight: 180 Origin: Round 11, 2017 Draft (#340 overall)

YEAR	TEAM	LVL	AGE	PA	R	2B	3B	HR	RBI	BB	K	SB	CS	AVG/OBP/SLG
2018	OGD	ROK	19	155	41	9	3	3	24	27	29	11	4	.346/.465/.535
2018	GL	LO-A	19	119	13	1	0	1	5	20	18	3	3	.265/.390/.306
2019	GL	LO-A	20	470	68	25	4	6	58	74	83	4	4	.262/.381/.394
2019	RC	HI-A	20	89	14	3	2	1	13	7	15	1	3	.250/.307/.375
2021 FS	LAD	MLB	22	600	52	23	3	8	52	58	161	2	3	.216/.297/.321

Comparables: Eugenio Suárez, Pete Kozma, Sean Rodríguez

He's underpowered, but infielder Jacob Amaya has good contact skills, doesn't expand his strike zone, and keeps his motor revved at higher RPM than a Trevor Bauer fastball.

YEAR	TEAM	LVL	AGE	PA	DRC+	BABIP	BRR	FRAA	WARP
2018	OGD	ROK	19	155		.432			
2018	GL	LO-A	19	119	130	.316	-1.8	SS(21): 2.2, 2B(5): -0.2	0.7
2019	GL	LO-A	20	470	145	.314	-0.5	SS(51): -3.8, 2B(49): 1.9, 3B(4): 0.1	3.6
2019	RC	HI-A	20	89	98	.292	0.3	SS(14): -2.1, 2B(4): 1.0, 3B(1): -0.0	0.2
2021 FS	LAD	MLB	22	600	72	.293	-0.3	SS 0, 2B 1	-0.3

Matt Beaty 1B

Born: 04/28/93 Age: 28 Bats: L Throws: R
Height: 6'0" Weight: 215 Origin: Round 12, 2015 Draft (#372 overall)

YEAR	TEAM	LVL	AGE	PA	R	2B	3B	HR	RBI	BB	K	SB	CS	AVG/OBP/SLG
2018	OKC	AAA	25	120	13	10	0	1	12	12	17	0	0	.277/.378/.406
2019	OKC	AAA	26	135	17	7	1	3	18	10	12	0	0	.306/.378/.455
2019	LAD	MLB	26	268	36	19	1	9	46	17	33	5	0	.265/.317/.458
2020	LAD	MLB	27	54	8	1	0	2	5	2	14	0	0	.220/.278/.360
2021 FS	LAD	MLB	28	600	76	32	1	18	79	39	115	1	1	.260/.319/.425
2021 DC	LAD	MLB	28	198	25	10	0	6	26	13	38	0	0	.260/.319/.425

Comparables: John Mabry, Greg Colbrunn, Robb Quinlan

There's a bunch of theoretical power upside here because Beaty has demonstrated the ability to generate high-end exit velocity, and he's just 28 in April. The gap between theory and practice can be considerable, though, and in Beaty's case, there are at least two reasons to be skeptical. One is the classic modern quandary: he mostly hits ground balls and low line drives. Launch angles are easy enough to fix, though, especially if you play for the Dodgers. That introduces the other problem: Beaty has a massive hole in his swing. Get it anywhere on the inner third or off the plate inside and he's tied in knots.

YEAR	TEAM	LVL	AGE	PA	DRC+	BABIP	BRR	FRAA	WARP
2018	OKC	AAA	25	120	109	.321	-0.3	1B(16): -0.3, LF(5): 1.0, 2B(4): -0.1	0.3
2019	OKC	AAA	26	135	92	.321	-0.4	1B(11): -0.9, 3B(11): 1.4, LF(8): 1.0	0.3
2019	LAD	MLB	26	268	93	.275	1.1	1B(35): -0.7, LF(34): 0.6, 3B(9): -0.5	0.5
2020	LAD	MLB	27	54	81	.265	-0.3	1B(13): -0.8, LF(2): 0.2	-0.1
2021 FS	LAD	MLB	28	600	100	.299	-0.9	LF 3, 3B -1	1.3
2021 DC	LAD	MLB	28	198	100	.299	-0.3	LF 1, 3B 0	0.5

Los Angeles Dodgers 2021

Michael Busch 2B
Born: 11/09/97 Age: 23 Bats: L Throws: R
Height: 6'0" Weight: 207 Origin: Round 1, 2019 Draft (#31 overall)

YEAR	TEAM	LVL	AGE	PA	R	2B	3B	HR	RBI	BB	K	SB	CS	AVG/OBP/SLG
2019	DOD1	ROK	21	16	1	0	0	0	0	1	2	0	0	.077/.250/.077
2019	GL	LO-A	21	19	4	0	0	0	2	6	3	0	0	.182/.474/.182
2021 FS	LAD	MLB	23	600	52	22	2	10	53	47	173	2	2	.205/.279/.315

Comparables: Santiago Espinal, Rafael Ynoa, Mark Canha

You don't have to squint that hard to see a Max Muncy future for Busch. In fact, that might undersell him if he continues on this trajectory. A first-round pick in 2019, Busch has hit (and hit good pitching) at absolutely every level at which he's been evaluated. His swing has easy lift and plenty of explosion. He spent the downtime (due to COVID-19) focusing on his quickness and athleticism, which figure to increase his chances of sticking at second base. Slide a slugging, disciplined college first baseman with a compact swing just that little bit up the defensive spectrum, and he becomes a stud prospect.

YEAR	TEAM	LVL	AGE	PA	DRC+	BABIP	BRR	FRAA	WARP
2019	DOD1	ROK	21	16		.091			
2019	GL	LO-A	21	19	132	.222	0.6	2B(4): 0.2	0.2
2021 FS	LAD	MLB	23	600	66	.279	-0.4	2B 2	-0.7

Diego Cartaya C
Born: 09/07/01 Age: 19 Bats: R Throws: R
Height: 6'2" Weight: 199 Origin: International Free Agent, 2018

YEAR	TEAM	LVL	AGE	PA	R	2B	3B	HR	RBI	BB	K	SB	CS	AVG/OBP/SLG
2019	DOD2	ROK	17	150	25	10	0	3	13	11	31	1	0	.296/.353/.437
2019	DSL BAU	ROK	17	57	11	2	2	1	9	5	11	0	0	.240/.316/.420
2021 FS	LAD	MLB	19	600	43	18	2	8	47	29	202	0	1	.188/.233/.274

Comparables: Bryan Anderson, Luis Campusano, Miguel Gonzalez

Demonstrating considerable trust in his touted makeup and dedication to catching, the Dodgers brought Cartaya to their alternate site to help handle a valuable, veteran pitching corps. It was the natural choice, not only because the team invested heavily in him as a top-billed Venezuelan signee in 2018, but because he's physically and mentally beyond his years. With a tall and powerful frame as well as a surprisingly controlled swing, Cartaya looks likely to knock on the door of the majors at a younger age than most catchers do.

YEAR	TEAM	LVL	AGE	PA	DRC+	BABIP	BRR	FRAA	WARP
2019	DOD2	ROK	17	150		.359			
2019	DSL BAU	ROK	17	57		.282			
2021 FS	LAD	MLB	19	600	38	.275	-0.6	C 0	-2.4

Kody Hoese 3B
Born: 07/13/97   Age: 23   Bats: R   Throws: R
Height: 6'4"   Weight: 200   Origin: Round 1, 2019 Draft (#25 overall)

YEAR	TEAM	LVL	AGE	PA	R	2B	3B	HR	RBI	BB	K	SB	CS	AVG/OBP/SLG
2019	DOD2	ROK	21	68	14	5	1	3	13	10	11	1	0	.357/.456/.643
2019	GL	LO-A	21	103	15	3	1	2	16	8	14	0	0	.264/.330/.385
2021 FS	LAD	MLB	23	600	50	23	2	9	53	41	156	0	1	.216/.277/.320

Comparables: Ty Kelly, Rangel Ravelo, Kelvin Gutierrez

When a pandemic hits and opportunities start drying up, it pays to be someone in whom your organization has already made a heavy investment. A 2019 first-round pick, Hoese was a priority assignee to the alternate site, and when that closed down, he moved right on to the fall instructional league in Arizona. No Dodgers swing path magic is needed here; Hoese already has leverage and lift, to go along with plenty of strength and fluid athleticism in his swing. They're always looking for a developmental twist to wring a little extra value out of a player though, which is how Hoese came to split his time between third base and shortstop. (Put nothing past this organization; they are the original and quintessential coconut snatchers.) He impressed on every level and against all the competition he could find in 2020.

YEAR	TEAM	LVL	AGE	PA	DRC+	BABIP	BRR	FRAA	WARP
2019	DOD2	ROK	21	68		.395			
2019	GL	LO-A	21	103	102	.286	-0.2	3B(12): 0.7	0.3
2021 FS	LAD	MLB	23	600	65	.284	-0.5	3B 0	-1.7

Gavin Lux 2B

Born: 11/23/97   Age: 23   Bats: L   Throws: R
Height: 6'2"   Weight: 190   Origin: Round 1, 2016 Draft (#20 overall)

YEAR	TEAM	LVL	AGE	PA	R	2B	3B	HR	RBI	BB	K	SB	CS	AVG/OBP/SLG
2018	RC	HI-A	20	404	64	23	7	11	48	43	68	11	7	.324/.396/.520
2018	TUL	AA	20	120	21	4	1	4	9	14	20	2	2	.324/.408/.495
2019	TUL	AA	21	291	45	7	4	13	37	28	60	7	3	.313/.375/.521
2019	OKC	AAA	21	232	54	18	4	13	39	33	42	3	3	.392/.478/.719
2019	LAD	MLB	21	82	12	4	1	2	9	7	24	2	0	.240/.305/.400
2020	LAD	MLB	22	69	8	2	0	3	8	6	19	1	0	.175/.246/.349
2021 FS	LAD	MLB	23	600	82	25	4	22	79	55	164	6	3	.252/.324/.438
2021 DC	LAD	MLB	23	524	72	22	3	19	69	48	143	5	3	.252/.324/.438

Comparables: Yu Chang, Daniel Robertson, Franchy Cordero

Don't read too much into Lux's struggles in extremely limited action across two fragmented seasons of big-league action. He has to make some adjustments—a second swing for when he can anticipate being attacked at the top of the zone, more balance in his swing and a cleaner transfer of energy from back to front side, things players only add to their games once the competition forces them to do so—but the pieces of a superstar all remain. He's excellent at second base and will be more than adequate if he's needed at shortstop again. He runs well. Once he cleans up his minor approach issues, he'll have consistently average-plus power. His circumstances have made his development seem rockier than it really is.

YEAR	TEAM	LVL	AGE	PA	DRC+	BABIP	BRR	FRAA	WARP
2018	RC	HI-A	20	404	145	.374	-1.8	SS(66): -0.6, 2B(17): 0.8	2.2
2018	TUL	AA	20	120	149	.370	1.3	SS(26): -0.6	0.9
2019	TUL	AA	21	291	166	.358	-2.6	SS(55): -3.0, 2B(7): 0.5	2.4
2019	OKC	AAA	21	232	176	.451	-1.2	SS(36): -2.8, 2B(12): -0.3	2.7
2019	LAD	MLB	21	82	74	.327	0.1	2B(22): -0.9	-0.1
2020	LAD	MLB	22	69	87	.195	0.2	2B(18): 2.2	0.3
2021 FS	LAD	MLB	23	600	105	.322	0.3	2B 2, SS 0	2.4
2021 DC	LAD	MLB	23	524	105	.322	0.3	2B 1	2.0

Zach McKinstry 2B

Born: 04/29/95 Age: 26 Bats: L Throws: R
Height: 6'0" Weight: 180 Origin: Round 33, 2016 Draft (#1001 overall)

YEAR	TEAM	LVL	AGE	PA	R	2B	3B	HR	RBI	BB	K	SB	CS	AVG/OBP/SLG
2018	GL	LO-A	23	72	12	2	2	3	8	16	16	2	1	.377/.542/.660
2018	RC	HI-A	23	114	20	7	1	2	8	17	22	0	0	.308/.447/.473
2018	TUL	AA	23	87	7	2	1	2	8	4	21	0	0	.193/.230/.313
2019	TUL	AA	24	384	53	16	4	12	52	37	74	8	8	.279/.352/.455
2019	OKC	AAA	24	95	17	8	2	7	26	6	18	0	1	.382/.421/.753
2020	LAD	MLB	25	7	1	1	0	0	0	0	3	0	0	.286/.286/.429
2021 FS	LAD	MLB	26	600	78	22	3	18	71	55	173	3	2	.227/.308/.385
2021 DC	LAD	MLB	26	218	28	8	1	6	25	20	62	0	1	.227/.308/.385

Comparables: Rougned Odor, German Duran, Cesar Hernandez

If the season had lasted 162 games, with the vagaries and attrition inherent to a schedule of that length, McKinstry would have gotten a more meaningful look in 2020. He's precisely the kind of player whom the Dodgers are adept at developing: a versatile, sure-handed infielder with a sneakily sound left-handed bat. He doesn't have Max Muncy-like power, nor the prospect sheen of a Gavin Lux or Corey Seager, but McKinstry has already added both bat speed and loft since joining the Los Angeles system, and he seems primed to take on a bigger role as a utility man in 2021.

YEAR	TEAM	LVL	AGE	PA	DRC+	BABIP	BRR	FRAA	WARP
2018	GL	LO-A	23	72	191	.500	-0.7	SS(11): -1.2, 2B(5): 0.1, LF(1): -0.1	0.7
2018	RC	HI-A	23	114	124	.388	0.3	2B(17): -0.5, 3B(5): 1.7, SS(5): -0.1	0.5
2018	TUL	AA	23	87	54	.233	-0.2	3B(14): 0.8, 2B(9): 0.5, SS(2): -0.2	-0.2
2019	TUL	AA	24	384	146	.323	-0.5	2B(49): -2.7, SS(29): 1.8, 3B(10): -0.1	2.7
2019	OKC	AAA	24	95	152	.422	-0.4	SS(17): -0.1, 2B(3): 0.4, 3B(2): 0.2	1.0
2020	LAD	MLB	25	7	69	.500		2B(1): -0.0, RF(1): 0.1	0.0
2021 FS	LAD	MLB	26	600	89	.299	-0.2	SS 1, 2B 0	1.2
2021 DC	LAD	MLB	26	218	89	.299	-0.1	SS 0, 2B 0	0.4

DJ Peters CF

Born: 12/12/95 Age: 25 Bats: R Throws: R
Height: 6'6" Weight: 225 Origin: Round 4, 2016 Draft (#131 overall)

YEAR	TEAM	LVL	AGE	PA	R	2B	3B	HR	RBI	BB	K	SB	CS	AVG/OBP/SLG
2018	TUL	AA	22	559	79	23	3	29	60	45	192	1	2	.236/.320/.473
2019	TUL	AA	23	288	31	10	1	11	42	27	93	1	0	.241/.329/.422
2019	OKC	AAA	23	255	40	10	1	12	39	33	74	1	1	.260/.388/.490
2021 FS	LAD	MLB	25	600	71	20	2	16	63	48	229	0	1	.197/.280/.334
2021 DC	LAD	MLB	25	103	12	3	0	2	10	8	39	0	0	.197/.280/.334

Comparables: Corey Brown, Matthew den Dekker, Wil Myers

He's a gym rat. He's a cage rat. He's coachable, he's personable, and he's downright Brobdingnagian. It's just not clear that Peters is going to make enough contact for all of that to matter.

YEAR	TEAM	LVL	AGE	PA	DRC+	BABIP	BRR	FRAA	WARP
2018	TUL	AA	22	559	95	.316	-3.6	CF(96): -3.1, RF(29): 1.4, LF(4): 0.1	-0.4
2019	TUL	AA	23	288	104	.331	-0.6	CF(48): -1.2, RF(20): 1.1	0.9
2019	OKC	AAA	23	255	120	.339	0.0	CF(56): -0.9	1.4
2021 FS	LAD	MLB	25	600	70	.307	-0.6	CF 1, LF 0	-0.5
2021 DC	LAD	MLB	25	103	70	.307	-0.1	CF 0	-0.1

Rangel Ravelo 1B
Born: 04/24/92 Age: 29 Bats: R Throws: R
Height: 6'1" Weight: 235 Origin: Round 6, 2010 Draft (#188 overall)

YEAR	TEAM	LVL	AGE	PA	R	2B	3B	HR	RBI	BB	K	SB	CS	AVG/OBP/SLG
2018	MEM	AAA	26	399	57	19	2	13	67	42	49	0	1	.308/.392/.487
2019	MEM	AAA	27	381	50	20	1	12	56	37	61	0	1	.299/.383/.473
2019	STL	MLB	27	43	4	2	0	2	7	3	12	0	0	.205/.256/.410
2020	STL	MLB	28	41	5	1	0	1	6	4	6	0	0	.171/.244/.286
2021 FS	LAD	MLB	29	600	64	24	1	18	68	52	128	0	1	.239/.317/.396

Comparables: Steve Pearce, Chris Marrero, Chris Carter

Ravelo has minimal power but makes contact and gets on base, which would be fine if he were a smooth left-handed second baseman instead of either a stiff right-handed first baseman or the short side of a DH platoon.

YEAR	TEAM	LVL	AGE	PA	DRC+	BABIP	BRR	FRAA	WARP
2018	MEM	AAA	26	399	136	.328	0.6	1B(54): 3.6, LF(36): -1.7, RF(1): 0.1	2.1
2019	MEM	AAA	27	381	118	.336	-0.3	1B(43): 1.4, LF(36): 2.9, 3B(5): -0.1	1.9
2019	STL	MLB	27	43	76	.231	-0.1	1B(9): -0.5	-0.1
2020	STL	MLB	28	41	91	.167	0.3	RF(4): -0.6, 1B(3): -0.1, LF(1): 0.1	0.1
2021 FS	LAD	MLB	29	600	100	.278	-0.9	1B 1, LF 1	1.3

Zach Reks LF

Born: 11/12/93 Age: 27 Bats: L Throws: R
Height: 6'2" Weight: 190 Origin: Round 10, 2017 Draft (#310 overall)

YEAR	TEAM	LVL	AGE	PA	R	2B	3B	HR	RBI	BB	K	SB	CS	AVG/OBP/SLG
2018	RC	HI-A	24	38	8	3	1	2	7	1	5	1	0	.405/.421/.703
2018	TUL	AA	24	296	37	14	1	3	33	34	73	5	3	.288/.368/.385
2019	TUL	AA	25	133	29	2	1	9	22	15	27	1	1	.310/.394/.584
2019	OKC	AAA	25	385	57	19	1	19	71	48	104	2	0	.284/.382/.520
2021 FS	LAD	MLB	27	600	79	24	1	17	71	54	178	1	1	.237/.315/.385
2021 DC	LAD	MLB	27	34	4	1	0	0	4	3	10	0	0	.237/.315/.385

Comparables: Jason Botts, John-Ford Griffin, Andrew Lambo

He's already 27 and just now clawed his way onto a 40-man roster, but Zach Reks is a lefty batter who can generate power and won't get himself out, so he's got a chance to hang around a bit.

YEAR	TEAM	LVL	AGE	PA	DRC+	BABIP	BRR	FRAA	WARP
2018	RC	HI-A	24	38	177	.433	0.7	1B(4): -0.5, LF(1): -0.2	0.3
2018	TUL	AA	24	296	107	.387	-2.4	LF(22): 0.0, RF(11): 0.3, 1B(6): -0.7	-0.2
2019	TUL	AA	25	133	189	.329	1.3	LF(19): -0.8, 1B(6): -0.8	1.3
2019	OKC	AAA	25	385	113	.359	0.9	LF(77): -3.8	1.3
2021 FS	LAD	MLB	27	600	91	.323	-0.8	LF 1, 1B 0	0.8
2021 DC	LAD	MLB	27	34	91	.323	0.0	LF 0	0.1

Los Angeles Dodgers 2021

Keibert Ruiz C
Born: 07/20/98 Age: 22 Bats: S Throws: R
Height: 6'0" Weight: 225 Origin: International Free Agent, 2015

YEAR	TEAM	LVL	AGE	PA	R	2B	3B	HR	RBI	BB	K	SB	CS	AVG/OBP/SLG
2018	TUL	AA	19	415	44	14	0	12	47	26	33	0	1	.268/.328/.401
2019	TUL	AA	20	310	33	9	0	4	25	28	21	0	0	.254/.329/.330
2019	OKC	AAA	20	40	6	0	0	2	9	2	1	0	0	.316/.350/.474
2020	LAD	MLB	21	8	1	0	0	1	1	0	3	0	0	.250/.250/.625
2021 FS	LAD	MLB	22	600	78	26	1	18	74	35	106	0	1	.261/.311/.415
2021 DC	LAD	MLB	22	62	8	2	0	1	7	3	10	0	0	.261/.311/.415

Comparables: Ryan Sweeney, Jake Bauers, Michael Brantley

Ruiz was sidelined by COVID-19 just before the resumption of spring training. His symptoms were (relatively) mild and he bounced back well, but the time in isolation as well as the lost weight and conditioning were unfriendly, even to a player whom some scouts had wished would slim down a bit. Once he reached the alternate site, Ruiz continued work he'd been doing before the interregnum, as he and three Dodgers coaches worked to unlock the power in his lower half. His setup in the box is unorthodox, but his swing has become steadily more smooth and modern over the last few years and the tumblers seemed to fall into place as 2020 progressed. He briefly reached the majors—homering in his first at-bat—and should be back sometime in 2021, as a sturdy, well-rounded catcher.

YEAR	TEAM	P. COUNT	FRM RUNS	BLK RUNS	THRW RUNS	TOT RUNS
2018	TUL	12404	5.3	-0.6	-0.4	4.2
2019	TUL	8965	3.3	0.0	-2.2	1.2
2020	LAD	315	-0.1	0.0	0.0	-0.1
2021	LAD	2405	-0.5	0.4	-0.1	-0.1
2021	LAD	2405	-0.5	0.1	-0.1	-0.5

YEAR	TEAM	LVL	AGE	PA	DRC+	BABIP	BRR	FRAA	WARP
2018	TUL	AA	19	415	92	.266	-3.8	C(86): 3.5	0.5
2019	TUL	AA	20	310	104	.261	-3.5	C(61): 0.5	1.1
2019	OKC	AAA	20	40	87	.286	0.9	C(9): -0.5	0.2
2020	LAD	MLB	21	8	91	.250		C(2): -0.0	0.0
2021 FS	LAD	MLB	22	600	97	.292	-0.9	C -1	2.0
2021 DC	LAD	MLB	22	62	97	.292	-0.1	C 0	0.2

Miguel Vargas 3B

Born: 11/17/99 Age: 21 Bats: R Throws: R
Height: 6'3" Weight: 205 Origin: International Free Agent, 2017

YEAR	TEAM	LVL	AGE	PA	R	2B	3B	HR	RBI	BB	K	SB	CS	AVG/OBP/SLG
2018	OGD	ROK	18	103	25	11	1	2	22	8	13	6	1	.394/.447/.596
2018	DOD2	ROK	18	37	6	3	1	0	2	5	3	1	0	.419/.514/.581
2018	GL	LO-A	18	89	4	1	1	0	6	10	20	0	0	.213/.307/.253
2019	GL	LO-A	19	323	53	20	2	5	45	35	43	9	1	.325/.399/.464
2019	RC	HI-A	19	236	23	18	1	2	32	20	40	4	3	.284/.353/.408
2021 FS	LAD	MLB	21	600	53	25	2	9	55	42	142	2	2	.235/.295/.344

Comparables: Matt Dominguez, Mike Moustakas, Rafael Devers

With a father who became a legend in Cuban baseball, great pure hitting skills, and a dearth of non-batting value, Vargas is shaping up to be Yuli Gurriel redux.

YEAR	TEAM	LVL	AGE	PA	DRC+	BABIP	BRR	FRAA	WARP
2018	OGD	ROK	18	103		.443			
2018	DOD2	ROK	18	37		.464			
2018	GL	LO-A	18	89	68	.281	-0.5	3B(19): 3.1	0.1
2019	GL	LO-A	19	323	162	.363	-2.5	3B(59): 2.2, 1B(2): 0.4, 2B(2): 0.4	3.1
2019	RC	HI-A	19	236	127	.341	-2.3	3B(43): -1.9, 1B(6): 0.4	0.8
2021 FS	LAD	MLB	21	600	75	.299	-0.4	3B 0, 1B 0	-0.8

Jake Vogel OF

Born: 10/12/01 Age: 19 Bats: R Throws: R
Height: 5'11" Weight: 165 Origin: Round 3, 2020 Draft (#100 overall)

An overslot high-school draftee, Vogel has excellent speed, a swing that already flashes good power and an advanced eye at the plate, which he showed off against advanced competition at the Dodgers' alternate site.

Clayton Beeter RHP

Born: 10/09/98 Age: 22 Bats: R Throws: R
Height: 6'2" Weight: 220 Origin: Round 2, 2020 Draft (#66 overall)

A second-round pick, Beeter has three plus offerings and a name that would make him the Dodgers' best starter ever, but he's already wearing two surgical scars.

Los Angeles Dodgers 2021

Gerardo Carrillo RHP
Born: 09/13/98 Age: 22 Bats: R Throws: R
Height: 5'10" Weight: 154 Origin: International Free Agent, 2016

YEAR	TEAM	LVL	AGE	W	L	SV	G	GS	IP	H	HR	BB/9	K/9	K	GB%	BABIP
2018	DOD2	ROK	19	2	0	1	4	1	11	6	0	1.6	10.6	13	57.7%	.231
2018	GL	LO-A	19	2	1	0	9	9	49	35	3	2.8	6.8	37	49.6%	.235
2019	RC	HI-A	20	5	9	0	23	21	86	87	3	5.3	9.0	86	54.2%	.339
2021 FS	LAD	MLB	22	2	3	0	57	0	50	48	7	4.8	7.5	41	46.9%	.283

Comparables: Rony García, Rob Kaminsky, Junior Fernández

Carrillo could be a good reliever, but if he cleans up his mechanics in the way other young Dodgers recently have, he might even stick as a solid starter.

YEAR	TEAM	LVL	AGE	WHIP	ERA	DRA-	WARP	MPH	FB%	WHF	CSP
2018	DOD2	ROK	19	0.73	0.82						
2018	GL	LO-A	19	1.02	1.65	80	0.9				
2019	RC	HI-A	20	1.60	5.44	107	-0.2				
2021 FS	LAD	MLB	22	1.50	5.06	116	-0.2				

Josiah Gray RHP
Born: 12/21/97 Age: 23 Bats: R Throws: R
Height: 6'1" Weight: 190 Origin: Round 2, 2018 Draft (#72 overall)

YEAR	TEAM	LVL	AGE	W	L	SV	G	GS	IP	H	HR	BB/9	K/9	K	GB%	BABIP
2018	GRN	ROK	20	2	2	0	12	12	52^1	29	1	2.9	10.1	59	36.4%	.219
2019	GL	LO-A	21	1	0	0	5	5	23^1	13	0	2.7	10.0	26	37.0%	.241
2019	RC	HI-A	21	7	0	0	12	12	67^1	52	3	1.7	10.7	80	36.3%	.293
2019	TUL	AA	21	3	2	0	9	8	39^1	33	0	2.5	9.4	41	34.3%	.317
2021 FS	LAD	MLB	23	2	2	0	57	0	50	43	6	3.7	8.7	48	35.8%	.276
2021 DC	LAD	MLB	23	1	1	0	27	0	27.7	24	3	3.7	8.7	26	35.8%	.276

Comparables: Yohander Méndez, Brett Cecil, Carl Edwards Jr.

The Dodgers insist that the controlled, collaborative (more than competitive) setting of the alternate site actually helped Gray, whose rising fastball is just too effective (and too much fun) to stop throwing when he has the chance (need) to win a ballgame. Reports say Gray's plus slider grew more consistent and his feel for his changeup improved as he threw both pitches (plus a curveball) more often than he might have otherwise. All that said, the lost season means we still need some answers. Gray's fastball velocity fluctuates a lot. Game settings at the upper levels will help show how he holds his velo as starts progress, where he's going to sit with the heat and whether the added confidence in his secondary stuff can make everything play up.

YEAR	TEAM	LVL	AGE	WHIP	ERA	DRA-	WARP	MPH	FB%	WHF	CSP
2018	GRN	ROK	20	0.88	2.58						
2019	GL	LO-A	21	0.86	1.93	46	0.8				
2019	RC	HI-A	21	0.97	2.14	47	2.2				
2019	TUL	AA	21	1.12	2.75	67	0.8				
2021 FS	LAD	MLB	23	1.28	3.67	89	0.5				
2021 DC	LAD	MLB	23	1.28	3.67	89	0.3				

Andre Jackson   RHP

Born: 05/01/96   Age: 25   Bats: R   Throws: R
Height: 6'3"   Weight: 210   Origin: Round 12, 2017 Draft (#370 overall)

YEAR	TEAM	LVL	AGE	W	L	SV	G	GS	IP	H	HR	BB/9	K/9	K	GB%	BABIP
2018	DOD2	ROK	22	2	0	0	4	3	18^1	18	0	2.0	15.2	31	40.0%	.450
2018	GL	LO-A	22	1	5	0	14	14	49^2	48	3	7.4	8.2	45	46.2%	.319
2019	GL	LO-A	23	4	1	0	10	10	48^1	29	1	3.5	9.3	50	46.7%	.237
2019	RC	HI-A	23	3	1	0	15	15	66^1	61	5	5.2	12.3	91	45.9%	.368
2021 FS	LAD	MLB	25	2	3	0	57	0	50	44	7	6.5	9.2	51	41.9%	.281

Comparables: Mike Montgomery, T.J. Zeuch, Alex Reyes

The sturdy, right-handed Jackson throws hard and registers good spin on his heat, but his changeup remains ahead of his breaking stuff.

YEAR	TEAM	LVL	AGE	WHIP	ERA	DRA-	WARP	MPH	FB%	WHF	CSP
2018	DOD2	ROK	22	1.20	3.44						
2018	GL	LO-A	22	1.79	4.35	153	-1.1				
2019	GL	LO-A	23	0.99	2.23	66	1.1				
2019	RC	HI-A	23	1.49	3.66	96	0.3				
2021 FS	LAD	MLB	25	1.61	5.05	114	-0.2				

Los Angeles Dodgers 2021

Tommy Kahnle RHP
Born: 08/07/89 Age: 31 Bats: R Throws: R
Height: 6'1" Weight: 230 Origin: Round 5, 2010 Draft (#175 overall)

YEAR	TEAM	LVL	AGE	W	L	SV	G	GS	IP	H	HR	BB/9	K/9	K	GB%	BABIP
2018	SWB	AAA	28	2	2	1	25	0	24^2	23	2	4.0	13.5	37	37.9%	.375
2018	NYY	MLB	28	2	0	1	24	0	23^1	23	3	5.8	11.6	30	38.7%	.339
2019	NYY	MLB	29	3	2	0	72	0	61^1	45	9	2.9	12.9	88	50.0%	.279
2020	NYY	MLB	30	0	0	0	1	0	1	1	0	9.0	27.0	3	100.0%	.500
2021 FS	LAD	MLB	31	2	2	0	57	0	50	40	5	4.2	11.9	66	45.2%	.300
2021 DC	LAD	MLB	31	2	2	0	52	0	45	36	5	4.2	11.9	59	45.2%	.300

Comparables: Jacob Barnes, Mychal Givens, Brad Boxberger

Middle relievers are essential components of a well-oiled modern baseball machine, but their absence is noticed more often than their presence. Kahnle made it into only one game in 2020 before being sidelined by forearm tightness that then led to the obligatory Tommy John surgery. His absence made the Yankees bullpen leaner, and in a year where starting pitchers weren't pushed nearly as hard because of an abbreviated ramp-up to a shortened season, that thinness impacted the team even more than it would have in a normal season. Kahnle could return in 2021 for the Dodgers, who inked him to a two-year pact over the winter, but that's only if he hits his most optimistic rehab targets.

YEAR	TEAM	LVL	AGE	WHIP	ERA	DRA-	WARP	MPH	FB%	WHF	CSP
2018	SWB	AAA	28	1.38	4.01	40	0.9				
2018	NYY	MLB	28	1.63	6.56	90	0.2	97.1	54.3%	34.9%	
2019	NYY	MLB	29	1.06	3.67	49	2.0	98.3	43.7%	36.6%	
2020	NYY	MLB	30	2.00	0.00	64	0.0	98.0	35.0%	66.7%	
2021 FS	LAD	MLB	31	1.28	3.38	79	0.8	98.1	45.6%	37.0%	47.2%
2021 DC	LAD	MLB	31	1.28	3.38	79	0.7	98.1	45.6%	37.0%	47.2%

C.C. Lee 李振昌 RHP

Born: 10/21/86 Age: 34 Bats: R Throws: R
Height: 5'11" Weight: 190 Origin:

YEAR	TEAM	LVL	AGE	W	L	SV	G	GS	IP	H	HR	BB/9	K/9	K	GB%	BABIP
2018	OKC	AAA	31	2	2	0	22	0	25[1]	17	3	3.2	14.6	41	42.3%	.286
2018	CTB	CPBL	31	1	0	14	28	0	27[1]	24	1	2.3	8.2	25		
2019	CTB	CPBL	32	3	1	10	54	0	52	43	2	0.9	11.4	66		
2020	CTB	CPBL	33	1	4	23	51	0	51[1]	33	6	2.6	13.7	78		
2021									No projection							

Comparables: Miguel Socolovich, Preston Guilmet, Brandon Gomes

Lee has some big league experience under his belt, throwing 34 innings for Cleveland from 2013 to 2015 after being signed out of Taiwan in 2008. After bouncing around the minors for a few years, with a 2016 stint on NPB's Seibu Lions mixed in, Lee made the decision to return to back home in 2018, and was picked in the first round (third overall) by the Brothers in that year's CPBL draft. Since then, he's been a lights-out closer, and his 13.7 K/9 in 2020 was a league-best. His streaks of dominance earned him the nickname "Instant Noodles Timer" around the league: start your instant noodles when Lee starts the ninth inning, and they still won't be done in the time it takes him to finish the game.

YEAR	TEAM	LVL	AGE	WHIP	ERA	DRA-	WARP	MPH	FB%	WHF	CSP
2018	OKC	AAA	31	1.03	3.91	19	1.2				
2018	CTB	CPBL	31	1.13	1.65						
2019	CTB	CPBL	32	0.92	1.21						
2020	CTB	CPBL	33	0.94	3.86						
2021					No projection						

Los Angeles Dodgers 2021

Bobby Miller   RHP
Born: 04/05/99   Age: 22   Bats: L   Throws: R
Height: 6'5"   Weight: 220   Origin: Round 1, 2020 Draft (#29 overall)

Is "a gigantic Walker Buehler" a fair comp to throw on anyone? Have you ever heard of Betteridge's Law of headlines? It also applies to first sentences of BP Annual player comments. Still, Miller is exciting. He's big and thickly built, but with the bouncy explosion and fiery demeanor Buehler brings to the mound. His fastball sits in the upper 90s and can show either heavy action at the bottom of the zone or rise at the top of it. He's worked to flesh out two distinct sliders (one more cutter than true slider) and two changeups (one a split-change). Best of all, though, the Dodgers were able to make him their first-round pick with confidence—despite the limited looks afforded by the COVID spring—thanks to the trust they have in scout Marty Lamb, who's been in their organization for over 20 years and whose Midwest coverage area has netted the team a fistful of recent top draftees. Holding onto and valuing veteran scouts pays off for the teams wise enough to do so.

David Price   LHP
Born: 08/26/85   Age: 35   Bats: L   Throws: L
Height: 6'5"   Weight: 215   Origin: Round 1, 2007 Draft (#1 overall)

YEAR	TEAM	LVL	AGE	W	L	SV	G	GS	IP	H	HR	BB/9	K/9	K	GB%	BABIP
2018	BOS	MLB	32	16	7	0	30	30	176	151	25	2.6	9.1	177	40.2%	.275
2019	BOS	MLB	33	7	5	0	22	22	107^1	109	15	2.7	10.7	128	41.0%	.336
2021 FS	LAD	MLB	35	9	8	0	26	26	150	141	25	2.5	9.0	149	40.2%	.288
2021 DC	LAD	MLB	35	7	6	0	25	21	111.3	105	18	2.5	9.0	111	40.2%	.288

Comparables: Carlos Carrasco, Felix Hernandez, Johnny Cueto

As it turned out, relatively few big-league players got seriously sick due to the global pandemic that defined 2020. Nevertheless, there were several points at which it looked not only as though the season might be thwarted, but that a full-fledged breakout might steer the sport into crisis and worsen the national disaster that is COVID-19. There remains an argument that playing the season did the latter. Price, who will put well over $200 million in the bank during his career even after accounting for the choice to surrender his 2020 paycheck, made the best choice for his family by opting out of the campaign. He's likely to pitch for the Dodgers for the first time in 2021, probably with a fresher arm, one fewer fastball, and (still) plenty of ways to get outs.

YEAR	TEAM	LVL	AGE	WHIP	ERA	DRA-	WARP	MPH	FB%	WHF	CSP
2018	BOS	MLB	32	1.14	3.58	83	3.2	94.5	46.6%	22.8%	
2019	BOS	MLB	33	1.31	4.28	96	1.3	94.1	52.0%	26.0%	
2021 FS	LAD	MLB	35	1.23	3.78	91	2.2	94.3	49.7%	24.7%	49.8%
2021 DC	LAD	MLB	35	1.23	3.78	91	1.7	94.3	49.7%	24.7%	49.8%

Mitch White   RHP

Born: 12/28/94   Age: 26   Bats: R   Throws: R
Height: 6'3"   Weight: 210   Origin: Round 2, 2016 Draft (#65 overall)

YEAR	TEAM	LVL	AGE	W	L	SV	G	GS	IP	H	HR	BB/9	K/9	K	GB%	BABIP
2018	TUL	AA	23	6	7	0	22	22	105^1	114	12	2.9	7.5	88	47.6%	.319
2019	TUL	AA	24	1	0	0	7	7	30	18	3	2.1	11.1	37	43.1%	.217
2019	OKC	AAA	24	3	6	0	16	13	63^2	73	13	3.4	9.6	68	41.6%	.351
2020	LAD	MLB	25	1	0	0	2	0	3	1	0	3.0	6.0	2	12.5%	.125
2021 FS	LAD	MLB	26	9	9	0	26	26	150	143	26	4.0	9.1	150	40.8%	.290
2021 DC	LAD	MLB	26	2	2	0	24	3	24	22	4	4.0	9.1	24	40.8%	.290

Comparables: Chase De Jong, Andrew Moore, Nabil Crismatt

It's nearly time to find out whether White's mid-90s heat will play up in relief. Maybe the Dodgers could give him a sinker, since they've become the leaders of a movement back to that recently-abandoned pitch. That would help establish some lateral separation between White's heat and his pair of breaking balls because, right now, there's not enough of it. Without that separation, he's heavily reliant on changing eye levels and commanding all three pitches. For a guy with a spotty health history and a track record of control outstripping command, that might be too heavy a lift.

YEAR	TEAM	LVL	AGE	WHIP	ERA	DRA-	WARP	MPH	FB%	WHF	CSP
2018	TUL	AA	23	1.41	4.53	108	0.0				
2019	TUL	AA	24	0.83	2.10	61	0.7				
2019	OKC	AAA	24	1.52	6.50	101	1.0				
2020	LAD	MLB	25	0.67	0.00	110	0.0	94.6	50.0%	22.7%	
2021 FS	LAD	MLB	26	1.41	4.56	105	1.0	94.6	50.0%	22.7%	42.3%
2021 DC	LAD	MLB	26	1.41	4.56	105	0.1	94.6	50.0%	22.7%	42.3%

Dodgers Prospects

The State of the System:
The depth and overall quality of the system has taken a dip from recent years. A lot of that has been because of graduated prospects who contributed to a World Series title, so you know, they're probably feeling okay on Vin Scully Ave.

The Top Ten:

1 ★ ★ ★ *2021 Top 101 Prospect* #55 ★ ★ ★
Josiah Gray **RHP** OFP: 60 ETA: 2021
Born: 12/21/97 Age: 23 Bats: R Throws: R Height: 6'1" Weight: 190
Origin: Round 2, 2018 Draft (#72 overall)

The Report: Gray was recruited to be primarily a shortstop at D-II LeMoyne College, albeit one that could throw a few innings here and there as well. By his junior year he was starting full time and dominating with a fastball that sat mid-90s. He's not a mere arm strength prospect at this point. Nor does he looks like a position player converted to the mound. Gray has a fluid, repeatable, uptempo delivery. He still sits mid-90s and both his slider and change have a chance to be above-average. There was some reliever risk coming out of college, but that was more due to demographics (cold weather arm, late pitching convert) than the idea that his stuff would especially play up in shorter bursts, and Gray might lack a true late-inning wipeout secondary, even though both have progressed well to this point. Now he just looks like a solid mid-rotation pitching prospect.

Development Track: Gray didn't look out of place in Dodgers instraquad games facing parts of … well, literally a World Series-winning lineup. He spent the balance of the summer at the alternate site to try and refine his secondaries, but he's about ready to be deployed in whatever role the Dodgers like, which I'd guess won't be a traditional 32 start /180 inning workhorse, but he'd likely be capable of that in time.

Variance: Medium. If Gray played for Kansas City or Miami, he probably would have seen time in the bigs and been able to acquit himself well enough. The Dodgers had pitching depth to spare in 2020, which does give Gray time to further tighten up his short, power slider and overall command.

Mark Barry's Fantasy Take: Typically "mid-rotation starter" is a term that is met with derision in fantasy circles. With Gray, however, I think his mid-rotation-ness (mid-rotation-osity?) stems more from organization and role than skill level. I like Gray quite a bit as a set-and-forget fantasy SP3-4, one capable of piling up strikeouts and wins, even if his spot in the rotation doesn't come with lofty innings totals.

★ ★ ★ *2021 Top 101 Prospect* **#74** ★ ★ ★

2

Keibert Ruiz   C   OFP: 60   ETA: Debuted in 2020
Born: 07/20/98   Age: 22   Bats: S   Throws: R   Height: 6'0"   Weight: 225
Origin: International Free Agent, 2015

The Report: Ruiz burst onto the prospect scene during the 2017 season, hitting .300 at two A-ball levels as an 18-year-old. The hit tool looked above-average, there was some raw power in the swing, and he was a precocious defender for his age. Wilson Karaman called him "a quality catching prospect with the ingredients to develop into a big-league starter, with room for a bit more if the right-handed swing maxes out." 2018 was more of the same, although an aggressive approach in Double-A cut into our confidence in the offensive tools. Kevin Carter liked the glove still: "His upside is tied to his approach and how much of his average raw power he taps into and with large improvements he could produce fringe-all-star value." Ruiz didn't really tame the aggressive approach in 2019—despite walking more than he struck out—and both the pop and quality of contact regressed. He added weight as well and Kevin now thought that: "All in all, his profile is starting to blur the line a bit between a major league regular projection and a quality tandem or backup."

There's a point to having as many citations here as Sam Fuld's Wikipedia page. Ruiz is six months younger than Adley Rutschman, but is a prime example of prospect fatigue, or perhaps John Sickels' Young Catcher Stagnation Syndrome. The development hasn't been along that nice y=x slope you'd want, and maybe some of his prospect helium was tied up in age-relative-to-league, but he still has potentially average offensive tools and above-average defensive ones. That's a good catching prospect, but one who still needs to take that next step, three years later.

Development Track: Ruiz got a couple games behind the plate while Will Smith was dealing with a neck issue and promptly hit a home run in his first major-league at-bat. That's pretty nice. However, his playing time may continue to be contingent on Will Smith's health, as the Dodgers' primary backstop looks like he might already be a top-five catcher in baseball, and his backup, Austin Barnes, is functionally Clayton Kershaw's personal catcher. Ruiz is only 22, and hasn't dominated the high minors yet, so he has a little more time to burn. He'll spend some of that time in 2021 hanging out in Oklahoma City, where we hope to see the bat take a step or two back forward.

Variance: High. Ruiz's prospect track has seen more fits and starts than you'd expect from a player about to make his fourth consecutive Top 101. The staff reports were downright mediocre in 2019, and while he appears to have righted the ship, there's still uncertainty around both the offensive and defensive parts of his game.

Mark Barry's Fantasy Take: As far as catching prospects are concerned, Ruiz is a pretty good one. The backstop hasn't seen a strikeout rate over 10 percent in any meaningful sample since 2017, which is certainly notable as batting averages dwindle league wide. Still, he's a catcher, and one who doesn't project to hit for much power. He's a top-200 guy, perhaps a little higher if you're in a two-catcher format.

─────── ★ ★ ★ *2021 Top 101 Prospect* **#77** ★ ★ ★ ───────

3 Miguel Vargas   3B   OFP: 60   ETA: 2022
Born: 11/17/99   Age: 21   Bats: R   Throws: R   Height: 6'3"   Weight: 205
Origin: International Free Agent, 2017

The Report: Vargas is a naturally gifted hitter with plus bat-to-ball ability and is able to drive the ball gap-to-gap, which has led to 53 doubles in just 177 minor league games. Advanced strike-zone awareness limits his strikeouts, prevents him from chasing bad pitches, and helped him establish a .387 career OBP. While his power has yet to fully develop, his sturdy base and strong physique are sure to produce more home runs as he matures. His mobility and range are somewhat limited, but Vargas has the soft hands and the arm strength to play a competent third base, while he also has seen time at first base or even second.

Development Track: Vargas didn't get an invite to the alternate site, but his offensive performance at instructs played to the pre-season scouting report. The body is on the high maintenance side now, but he still looked fine at the hot corner, although the Dodgers are already moving him around the infield some. Vargas would have been ticketed to start 2020 in Double-A and given the limited 2020 game time, I'd expect that to be his starting point in 2021. The bat is capable of forcing the issue if his power continues to develop, even given a crowded major-league roster.

Variance: Medium. Despite the limited action, the bat gives Vargas a high floor, although we'd feel better about everything if he spent 2020 conquering the upper minors.

Mark Barry's Fantasy Take: Plenty of patience and lots of contact, you say? Vargas' loud arrival on the dynasty scene was quieted only by, uh, not playing real games in 2020, an issue we'll hopefully get to rectify in 2021. This profile is one I really like, especially with budding power reaching maturity as he gets closer to a debut. Vargas still has something to prove, as he hasn't faced pitching above High-A, but he's probably flirting with the top-100 dynasty prospects right now, and could even tick higher in the future.

─────── ★ ★ ★ *2021 Top 101 Prospect* **#91** ★ ★ ★ ───────

4 **Michael Busch 2B**   OFP: 55   ETA: Late 2021/Early 2022
Born: 11/09/97   Age: 23   Bats: L   Throws: R   Height: 6'0"   Weight: 207
Origin: Round 1, 2019 Draft (#31 overall)

The Report: The Dodgers popped Busch at the end of the first round in 2019 based on the strength of his bat. He raked his junior year at UNC, and while he doesn't have the loudest offensive tools you'll see, he does everything well. Hit, approach, pop, everything is above-average. While the bat might have been worthy of going in the top half of the first round, Busch was primarily a 1B/LF in college. That's going to put a bit of a damper on the overall profile, but the Dodgers being the Dodgers, they made him a second baseman. So we will list him at the keystone, although I suspect he will play there in the same way Max Muncy does—on occasion and not particularly well.

Development Track: "Busch is awesome." The praise for his performance in instructs was effusive. He showed good feel for contact and control of the zone, with burgeoning power. The hit and power tools could both end up above-average or better. He has settled into second base and while he's unlikely to grade out as average there, it's playable. The bat might be good enough now that it doesn't matter where he stands.

Variance: Medium. Busch is going to hit, and should be good enough defensively that you're happy enough to have him in the lineup wherever. Still need to see him do it in the upper minors though, and the glove might eat into his value some.

Mark Barry's Fantasy Take: Speaking of the Dodgers player development, it seems like Busch's profile (read: patience, power, no defensive position) is one that typically thrives in the organization. He got next to zero run after being drafted in 2019, so there's a good chance he's still a little unheralded in the dynasty world. I think he's a top-125ish guy that could even sneak into that top-100 on my personal list.

5 **Diego Cartaya C**   OFP: 55   ETA: 2024
Born: 09/07/01   Age: 19   Bats: R   Throws: R   Height: 6'2"   Weight: 199
Origin: International Free Agent, 2018

The Report: The Dodgers put Cartaya on the Keibert Ruiz track of catching development. They aggressively brought him stateside at 17 as soon as the AZL started and he was living with their Triple-A manager and former roving catcher instructor, Travis Barbary, during the shutdown. The similarities end there though. Cartaya has more raw power projection and a potential plus hit tool, but the defensive game is not as advanced as it was for teenaged Ruiz. Cartaya lacks some of the quick-twitch actions a modern catcher is expected to have and his receiving is more brute strength than finesse at present. Some of that will smooth out with more professional instruction and reps, but the profile is hit-over-glove, and that doesn't always fly behind the plate. There's potential on both sides of the ball though.

Development Track: Cartaya got about the fullest 2020 a prospect could get, spending time at both the alternate site and instructs. Reports on the bat in Camelback were a bit muted, but it was an unusual season, and he was facing a better caliber arm than your usual instructional league crop. Cartaya just turned 19, but I'd expect given how aggressively the Dodgers have handled him that he will be ticketed for a full-season affiliate in 2021.

Variance: Extreme. The bat is ahead of the glove here, and the bat hasn't really been tested by better pitching yet.

Mark Barry's Fantasy Take: If you wanted to push Cartaya ahead of Ruiz on your personal list, I wouldn't begrudge you too much. Cartaya projects to have more power than his colleague behind the dish, and while his hit tool might not be as renowned as Ruiz's, it's still pretty solid. His defense will need to improve to stay at catcher, though, and if he doesn't stay at catcher, he's less interesting for fantasy purposes.

Bobby Miller   RHP   OFP: 55   ETA: 2023 as a starter, 2022 as a reliever
Born: 04/05/99   Age: 22   Bats: L   Throws: R   Height: 6'5"   Weight: 220
Origin: Round 1, 2020 Draft (#29 overall)

The Report: The other half of the best tandem of collegiate pitchers, Miller actually has the edge over his former Louisville teammate Reid Detmers in terms of dynamic stuff despite being picked 19 spots later in the first round. As our own Ben Spanier witnessed, Miller features a live fastball in the mid-90s that holds it's heat late into games and can ramp the pitch up to 99 at times. His ability to command it to either side of the plate gilds the lily further. He backs it up with a curling slider in the low 80s that is his second-best offering. A cutter and firm changeup round-out the mix, both needing to improve in order to reach average grades.

Development Track: Given Miller's athletic frame, there is a chance the fastball velocity can still find another gear, even though that's the least of concerns with the profile. The arm stroke is rather elongated, forcing his glove hand to reach out front to maintain balance. This makes his secondaries a little difficult to repeat. Already lacking finish on both the cutter and change, without improvement in the other two secondaries, there will be relief concerns. Having never spent an entire year as a starter while in school, he will need to prove his stuff can be sustained across an entire season.

Variance: High. There is a lot of potential in the arm that could blossom or stagnate. The requisite off-speed improvements may be difficult to make without adversely affecting the electric heater.

Mark Barry's Fantasy Take: A couple things worry me about Miller. First, he hasn't spent a full year as a starter. And second, he has two very good pitches, but the rest of the arsenal is underdeveloped. Usually that screams reliever. Too negative? Fine. First, he hasn't spent a full year as a starter, so he doesn't have the same wear and tear on his arm. And second, he's in a great organization for developing secondary offerings. Better? Good.

Keep Miller on the watchlist for now, or scoop him up in leagues with 200+ prospects.

7. Andre Jackson RHP   OFP: 50   ETA: Late 2021/Early 2022
Born: 05/01/96   Age: 25   Bats: R   Throws: R   Height: 6'3"   Weight: 210
Origin: Round 12, 2017 Draft (#370 overall)

The Report: A former college outfielder, the 6-foot-3 Jackson utilizes a high release point and a mid-90s fastball to consistently challenge hitters up in the zone. Pairing perfectly with the high heat is a plunging upper-70s curveball. His mid-80s changeup is a work in progress, but there has been progression. While Jackson's command will need to improve, his competitiveness will serve him well in either a starter or reliever role in the big leagues.

Development Track: The 24-year-old has learned and developed quickly while playing across four levels in two minor league seasons. While he may only start next season in Double-A, Jackson could appear in a Dodgers uniform as soon as 2021.

Variance: Medium. Improved command and fewer walks issued would expedite his big-league arrival.

Mark Barry's Fantasy Take: Jackson is probably a reliever, but his path to the doorstep of the big leagues has been anything but conventional, so there's still space to dream on his role. For now, he's a fringe-watchlist guy, but be sure to have that quick claim finger ready, should he pop as a starter in early 2021.

8. Kody Hoese 3B   OFP: 50   ETA: 2022
Born: 07/13/97   Age: 23   Bats: R   Throws: R   Height: 6'4"   Weight: 200
Origin: Round 1, 2019 Draft (#25 overall)

The Report: Hoese followed up a strong 2018 Cape Cod campaign with an outrageous junior year at Tulane. Nearly scraping .400 with 23 homers and more walks than strikeouts, he played his way into the first round of the draft. The power is plus, but it takes some length and leverage from his large, sturdy frame to tap into it, which can lead to swing-and-miss issues. The approach is solid enough in terms of knowing what to zone to get the most out of his pop, so the offensive profile may lean towards the Three True Outcomes. That's fine in an everyday third baseman, although Hoese is not a lock to stick there given his size and stiffness in the field.

Development Track: It's easy to pair Hoese and Busch as advanced college bats taken in the first round of the same draft, and a mere six spots apart at that. Hoese is more power-over-hit though, and despite having a more clear cut position, looked downright rusty at third in instructs. The reports on his defense have been decidedly mixed for a while, and Keanan had a 40 on the third base glove pre-2019 draft. Hoese looked more comfortable at shortstop this fall, but that's a stretch even for the Dodgers, so you hope the recent issues at the hot corner were just a product of the weirdness of player development in 2020. None of this matters if he continues to hit and hit for power mind you.

Variance: High. Hoese is 23 and has 22 games outside of college or the complex. There's hit tool and positional questions as well.

Mark Barry's Fantasy Take: For fantasy, I might have Hoese challenging Gray for the top spot on this list. Hoese made a bunch of contact in the small sample of his 2019 debut, and while that ultimately might not carry over against advanced pitching, his plate discipline and power should more than make up for any swing-and-miss in his profile. Lazy organizational comp coming: he's basically right-handed Max Muncy.

9. Jacob Amaya   SS   OFP: 50   ETA: 2022
Born: 09/03/98   Age: 22   Bats: R   Throws: R   Height: 6'0"   Weight: 180
Origin: Round 11, 2017 Draft (#340 overall)

The Report: Although Amaya might struggle to crack double-digit home runs, he's far from an offensive zero. He's a tough out due to his strong strike zone awareness and plus contact ability that he can work gap-to-gap. This has led him to run high OBPs, which should continue in the majors. Amaya can potentially pair that with a .280 batting average and plenty of doubles. A natural shortstop, his soft hands and strong arm will enable him to play all three infield positions at the highest level. His speed and baserunning savvy make him dangerous every time he makes his way to first.

Development Track: While he last played at the High-A level, Amaya's strong fundamentals and well-rounded game will allow him to progress quickly. Further development of his offensive skills would hasten his ascension to the show.

Variance: Medium. His broad base of offensive and defensive skills give him a bunch of ways to help your major league club, although the overall ceiling is somewhat limited.

Mark Barry's Fantasy Take: Amaya does a bunch of things pretty well, without doing anything *very* well. He should have a major-league role, but his fantasy usefulness might be limited to NL-only leagues.

10. Gerardo Carrillo   RHP   OFP: 50   ETA: 2022
Born: 09/13/98   Age: 22   Bats: R   Throws: R   Height: 5'10"   Weight: 154
Origin: International Free Agent, 2016

The Report: The 22-year-old right-hander has as electric an arm as any pitcher in the Dodgers organization. Emanating from a seemingly effortless motion, Carrillo's fastball sits comfortably in the high-90s and can reach triple-digits. His secondary offerings remain a work in progress, consisting of a slurvy breaking ball with varying velocity and shape, a high-80s changeup, and a hard cutter that he can work inside against lefties. He's sometimes struggled with command as a pro, but has also demonstrated the ability to make adjustments and improvements required to develop into a quality major-league hurler.

Development Track: Carrillo has yet to throw more than 86 innings in a professional season. While he's worked primarily as a starter in the minors, a transition to the bullpen is always an option for the hard-throwing righty.

Variance: High. The natural velocity is impressive, but Carrillo must refine his command and further develop his craft to become a successful big-leaguer.

Mark Barry's Fantasy Take: It would be nice to see Carillo consistently put together some heavy-inning workloads to assuage fears of a role spent in relief, but as it stands, he's probably just a reliever, and not terribly exciting for fantasy purposes.

The Prospects You Meet Outside The Top Ten

Almost an entire draft class

Landon Knack Born: 07/15/97 Age: 23 Bats: L Throws: R Height: 6'2" Weight: 220 Origin: Round 2, 2020 Draft (#60 overall)
Not your typical fifth-year senior sign, Knack had one of the most unique profiles in this year's draft. Due to injuries that cost him most of three different seasons while he was a two-way player, Knack has been a full-time pitcher for only a year, and the stuff dramatically improved over that period. With the lack of miles on the arm, the velocity already peaking in the mid-90s, potentially average secondary pitches, and very good control, there is a ton to build on here.

Clayton Beeter RHP Born: 10/09/98 Age: 22 Bats: R Throws: R Height: 6'2" Weight: 220 Origin: Round 2, 2020 Draft (#66 overall)
Injuries plagued Beeter throughout his senior year of high school and freshman year at Texas Tech, resulting in two elbow surgeries including Tommy John. Beeter returned as a reliever for his sophomore campaign in 2019 and struck out nearly two batters an inning. It was an effectively wild approach, though as he walked nearly a batter per as well. The dynamic arsenal was too good sequestered in the bullpen, so last spring he was given the chance to start, and made the most of his four starts. Even with the 2020 success, however abbreviated, the injury history is difficult to ignore, likely relegating him to a late-inning role to maximize his value. It's lights-out stuff that could play well in high leverage situations, featuring upper 90s heat and plus-plus slider.

Jake Vogel   OF   Born: 10/12/01   Age: 19   Bats: R   Throws: R   Height: 5'11"   Weight: 165   Origin: Round 3, 2020 Draft (#100 overall)

In the running—no pun intended—for fastest player in this year's prep class, the SoCal product had to be enticed by a well over-slot deal to sign with the Dodgers. Vogel garnered mixed reviews on his offensive potential, mostly because of his light frame and compact swing. That featherweight body allows for the elite foot-speed to play on the bases and especially in the outfield. The quick-twitch athleticism is what highlights the profile, with significant improvements to the swing necessary to reach his full potential.

Prospects to dream on a little

Andy Pages   RF   Born: 12/08/00   Age: 20   Bats: R   Throws: R   Height: 6'1"   Weight: 180   Origin: International Free Agent, 2018

Pages moves from Low Minors Sleeper to uh … Low Minors Prospect, I guess. He looked good at instructs, still every bit the potential plus hit/power combo he'll need to carry a corner outfield profile, but the lost year hurts here more than most.

Pitchers that are either good or unavailable, too often unavailable

Mitch White   RHP   Born: 12/28/94   Age: 26   Bats: R   Throws: R   Height: 6'3"   Weight: 210   Origin: Round 2, 2016 Draft (#65 overall)

White has long been a favorite of the west coast branch of our prospect team. Granted, that's mostly because they have been the only ones able to catch the about-to-be 26-year-old. And that's never been as frequently as they'd like. The various maladies have depleted the stuff at times, but the fastball is back to mid-90s in short bursts and he pairs it with an above-average slider/cutter thing and low-80s curve. He might just be a 95-and-a-breaking-ball guy, but at least he is healthy now as far as we know.

Michael Grove   RHP   Born: 12/18/96   Age: 24   Bats: R   Throws: R   Height: 6'3"   Weight: 200   Origin: Round 2, 2018 Draft (#68 overall)

Grove was coming off Tommy John surgery last year, so that at least explains his limited reps. He's worked on ironing out some of the mechanical issues we saw last year, and the fastball has ticked up to plus, and an improving change-up could get there as well. There's still a ways to go here, but signs are pointing in the right direction for Grove to be inside the Top 10 this time next year.

The Dodgers' next out of nowhere player development success story

Zach McKinstry   2B   Born: 04/29/95   Age: 26   Bats: L   Throws: R   Height: 6'0"   Weight: 180   Origin: Round 33, 2016 Draft (#1001 overall)

McKinstry was a 33rd rounder out of Central Michigan. A solid college performer whose best tool was his approach, he seemed destined to be the kind of player who bounced around a minor league bench for a few seasons before becoming a coach or an insurance adjuster. He slugged .295 in the Cal League in 2017. Come on now, you know how this ends. Well two years and one swing change later, McKinstry socked 19 home runs in the upper minors. He can play all over the diamond, and while the power might not reach the heights he found with the Triple-A ball in PCL parks, the Dodgers might not miss Enrique Hernandez as much as you'd think in 2021.

Top Talents 25 and Under (as of 4/1/2021):

1. Cody Bellinger, OF/1B
2. Dustin May, RHP
3. Gavin Lux, 2B
4. Julio Urías, LHP
5. Josiah Gray, RHP
6. Keibert Ruiz, C
7. Brusdar Graterol, RHP
8. Miguel Vargas, 3B
9. Michael Busch, 2B
10. Diego Cartaya, C

This is one of the most loaded crops of young major-league talent in the league, just in case you were worried that the Dodgers were going anywhere anytime soon. Kicking us off is Cody Bellinger, the 2019 National League MVP. Bellinger was not quite able to match his 8 WARP 2019 pace in 2020, with his batting average dropping from .305 to .239 in the shortened season. He was still really good, and he continued his move up the defensive spectrum by taking about two-thirds of his playing time in center. He's one of the best players in baseball and may not have hit his true peak yet.

The next three names could be in virtually any order. Dustin May was the No. 8 prospect in baseball entering last season, and the surprising Opening Night starter after Clayton Kershaw was a late scratch. He pitched most of the season in the rotation, working mostly off stupendous high-90s sinkers and low-90s cutters. He didn't miss as many bats as you'd expect given the velocity and movement, but he was extremely impressive.

Gavin Lux was the highest-rated prospect of this trio, topping out at No. 2 last offseason. The Dodgers seemed surprisingly uninterested in playing him in 2020, dispatching him to the alternate site long enough to not only claw back a year of service time but likely a year of Super 2 eligibility as well. He saw only partial playing time at second base down the stretch, and didn't even make the NLCS or World Series rosters. This was enough of a lost year to swap him with May, who wasn't much worse of a prospect and established himself as a good major-league pitcher, but we're still looking for Lux to be an offensive force starting very soon.

Julio Urías was the No. 6 prospect on the 101 five years ago. In the intervening years, he's still never actually thrown a full-length season between shoulder capsule surgery and workload concerns. He might never, but he's an extremely effective pitcher no matter the role, as you saw in the closing innings of Game 7 of the World Series.

The Dodgers picked up big righty Brusdar Graterol in the second version of the Mookie Betts deal. He was used in a wide variety of short roles in the regular season, from opener to the eighth inning and everywhere in between, before settling in as a primary setup man in the postseason. Graterol throws 100-plus regularly with a nasty slider, and if he continues along his present path he's going to be quite a fine reliever. We'd still like to see him get a shot at starting long-term, but it's hard to see him getting the opportunity given all of Los Angeles's pitching depth.

Two more non-prospect pitchers lurk just off the list and warrant a mention. Like Graterol, lefties Caleb Ferguson and Victor González are both starters by trade who have thrived airing it out in relief roles for the Dodgers. It is a huge competitive advantage to have enough pitching depth to let them do it.

Part 3: Featured Articles

Dodgers All-Time Top 10 Players

by Rob Mains

POSITION PLAYERS

ROY CAMPANELLA, C (1948-1957)
In his three MVP years—1951, 1953, and 1955—he hit .318/.394/.595 with 105 homers and 357 RBI. In the following three years, he hit .234/.325/.418. with 61 homers and 221 RBI. Beginning in 1954, a series of wrist and hand injuries limited his playing time, and then his career was tragically cut short by a January 1958 car accident that left him permanently paralyzed. The front end of his career was truncated as well; he played in the Negro Leagues from 1937 (when he was 15!) through 1945 and was a 25-year-old at Triple-A Montreal when Jackie Robinson broke the color line in 1947.

GIL HODGES, 1B (1943-1961)
Hodges is second in franchise history in homers (361) and RBI (1,254). His .847 Dodger OPS is fifth in team history among players with at least 3.000 plate appearances. He drove in 100 or more runs for seven straight seasons and drew at least 70 walks seven straight years as well. He was popular with the home crowd and had a successful career as a manager before suddenly dying of a heart attack at 47. Was temporarily saddled with the "choker" label after going 0-for-21 in the 1952 World Series, but hit well in his four remaining Fall Classics, hitting .337 in 26 games.

STEVE GARVEY, 1B (1969-1982)
Garvey was a third baseman when he broke into the majors but a bad throwing arm dictated a move across the diamond where he picked up four straight Gold Gloves. He had a .301 batting average for the Dodgers, made 200 or more base hits in six years, was part of a famous infield, and played in 1,207 straight games. He didn't walk a lot and had limited power for a first baseman, hitting more

than 25 homers only three times. He thus was, at various points in his career, overrated and underrated. Adjusting for Dodger Stadium and moderate scoring environment in which he played, his career .796 OPS was 22 percent above average, which is plenty good enough.

JACKIE ROBINSON, 2B (1947-1956)
It's not an overstatement to call him one of the most important people in American history, rendering his accomplishments on the field secondary. But he was a superlative ballplayer: An outstanding fielder, great baserunner (led the league in steals twice), and .311/.409/.474 lifetime average at a glove-first position. He had an OPS over .900 for six straight seasons. And he did all this despite not playing in the majors until he was 28.

JIM GILLIAM, 2B/3B (1953-1966)
All he had to do in his rookie year was displace Jackie Robinson at second base, pushing the legend to left field. He pulled it off, batting .278/.383/.415, walking 100 times, leading the league with 17 triples, and winning Rookie of the Year. He became a fixture atop Dodger lineups, always drawing plenty of walks (.360 career OBP), and finishing in the top 10 in the league in stolen bases nine times. He was impossible to strike out and rarely missed games. Perhaps his greatest skill was versatility; the Dodgers chose his position based on need and he always gave them an instant upgrade.

RON CEY, 3B (1971-1982)
The Penguin didn't have the media savvy of his across-the-diamond peer Garvey but he quietly amassed one of the greatest Dodger careers, ranking fifth in team history with 228 homers. Between 1973 and 1980, he averaged 154 games and 24 homers per year. His .264 batting average was bolstered by an LA Dodger-record 765 walks, yielding an .804 OPS that was 25 percent above average when adjusted for season and park. He never won a Gold Glove but was an above-average third baseman as well.

PEE WEE REESE, SS (1940-1958)
Reese is the franchise recordholder for runs and walks and is second in plate appearances and hits, all despite missing three full years to World War II. His ability to draw walks made him a good fit at the top of the order; despite a career .269 batting average his on-base percentage was an outstanding .366. He was in the top ten in the league in OBP five times and runs scored eight times. That, combined with an outstanding glove, earned the team captain MVP votes in twelve straight seasons.

ZACK WHEAT, OF (1909-1926)

The Brooklyn team was known as the Superbas, Dodgers, and Robins during Wheat's years with the club and, despite two World Series appearances, were mostly bad (5 winning seasons in his 18 years). Wheat was the team's best hitter and one of the top National League hitters of the Deadball Era. His .317 average is the highest in franchise history (min. 1,000 games) and his .819 OPS, adjusted for the era, is fifth-highest. All the introduction of the modern ball did was push him higher, allowing him to do things like hit .375/.428/.549 in 1924. He was considered the best-fielding outfielder of his era, stole 203 bases, and is the franchise leader for hits, singles, doubles, triples, and total bases.

DUKE SNIDER, OF (1947-1962)

The song "Willie, Mickey and the Duke" illustrates Snider's poor luck in playing in New York at the same time as arguably the two greatest center fielders of all time. As a Dodger, he hit an even .300 and is first in franchise history for slugging (.553), OPS (.936), homers (389), and RBI (1,271). From 1953 to 1955 he hit .329/.420/.634 and averaged 41 homers and 131 RBI per year while leading the league in runs scored each season. That the move west to the Los Angeles Coliseum with its insanely deep right field almost finished him is a legend—he hit .302/.383/.542 there. It just wasn't as favorable as the tiny Ebbets Field had been (.313/.396/.603) and age and injuries were taking their toll coincident to the move.

WILLIE DAVIS, OF (1960-1973)

Davis is one of the most underrated players in Dodgers history because he played during one of the lowest-scoring eras in baseball history in an extreme pitcher's park. He was an outstanding fielder, a devastating baserunner (third in franchise history with 335 stolen bases and second with 110 triples) and one of the best players on the dominant Dodgers teams of the early 1960s. He's the Los Angeles Dodger leader in hits and runs.

PITCHERS

NAP RUCKER, LHP (1907-1916)

The franchise's first great lefty was a workhorse from 1907 through 1913, averaging 42 games, 34 starts, and 302 innings per season, pitching the second-most innings in the league. He did this in service of Brooklyn teams that were below .500 every year, though, so his 2.39 ERA—21 percent better than average—yielded only a 116-123 record. All that work wore him down, though, and he managed only 264 more innings over his final three seasons, the last when he was only 31.

JEFF PFEFFER, RHP (1913-1921)

His Deadball-Era 2.31 ERA is the lowest in club history. He was known as "Big Jim," listed at 6-foot'3 and 210 pounds, huge for his era. He missed all but one game in 1918 due to service in the Navy, but in his six full seasons with the club he averaged 281 innings per year, posting a 111-74 record. He was consistently one of his teams' best pitchers and is among franchise leaders in complete games, shutouts, and lowest walk percentage.

DAZZY VANCE, RHP (1922-1932, 1935)

A failed prospect, Vance was almost forced on the Dodgers as the price for acquiring journeyman catcher Hank DeBerry from the minor league New Orleans Pelicans. Surprise: Pitching out of a tattered sleeve with great stuff, Vance led the league in strikeouts every year from 1922 to 1928, often by huge margins. In his MVP season of 1924—28 wins, 2.16 ERA, 30 complete games, all league-leading—he struck out 262 batters, a total that wouldn't be surpassed in the National League until Sandy Koufax whiffed 269 in 1961. His first season with Brooklyn wasn't until he was 32, but he was 190-131 with a 3.17 ERA for the Dodgers, third on the franchise win list, pitching mostly for sub-.500 team.

SANDY KOUFAX, LHP (1955-1966)

You probably know the story: League-average pitcher his first six years in the league, retired at 30 due to an arthritic elbow, and in between, as dominant as any pitcher's ever been. From 1961 to 1966, Koufax averaged a 22-8 record with a 2.19 ERA, starting 35 games and completing 19 over 272 innings. He led the league in strikeouts four times, ERA five times, wins three times, was MVP of two World Series. There was only one Cy Young Award for all of baseball when Koufax pitched, and in his last four years, he won it three times and finished third once. Did we mention the four no-hitters, one of them a perfect game?

DON DRYSDALE, RHP (1956-1969)

He's second in franchise history in starts, innings, and wins, yet his career was over when he was only 32 due to shoulder problems in 1969. Prior to that year, he averaged 37 starts and 273 innings per season over 12 years. He won the Cy Young Award in 1962, when he was 25-9 with a 2.83 ERA in 314 1/3 innings, and he famously set the record for consecutive shutouts, six, and consecutive scoreless innings, 58 2/3, in 1968. He led the league in strikeouts three times and teamed with Koufax to form one of the most formidable starting tandems in history.

DON SUTTON, RHP (1966-1980, 1988)

He pitched for 15 seasons in Los Angeles, topping 200 innings every year, then averaged 200+ per year for seven seasons with four other clubs before returning to LA in 1988, when he was 43. His nickname was "Black & Decker" because of constant accusations of scuffing the ball. He led the league with a 2.20 ERA in

1980 and was in the top ten in walks and hits per innings pitched 12 times. He's the franchise leader in starts (533), wins (233), innings (3,816 1/3), and strikeouts (2,696). He wasn't often spectacular, but consistency, especially at a high level, is a skill too.

BOB WELCH, RHP (1978-1987)

His most famous moment was his rookie-year strikeout of Reggie Jackson to end the second game of the 1978 World Series with the Dodgers clinging to a 4-3 lead and the A's threatening with runners on first and second. (Reggie got his revenge, singling off Welch in the tenth inning of Game 4, setting up the winning run, and hitting a two-run bomb off him in the series-clinching Game Six.) Welch's first season featured a 2.02 ERA in 111 innings. He also had developed a serious drinking problem, which almost derailed his career in 1979. He went into rehab and came back to become one of the team's most dependable starters, averaging 204 innings and a 3.17 ERA between 1980 and 1987, then went on to a Cy Young-winning third act with Oakland.

FERNANDO VALENZUELA, LHP (1980-1990)

During his rookie year of 1981, Fernandomania swept baseball. In the strike-shortened split season, he led the league in starts, complete games, shutouts, innings, and strikeouts, and was seventh in ERA (2.48). He was Rookie of the Year and Cy Young Award winner, drawing huge crowds wherever he pitched. He was 3-1 with a 2.21 ERA in 31 2/3 postseason innings. He was also only 20, and heavy workloads over his next six seasons as well (averaging 266 innings and 3.19 ERA, average 16-12 record) robbed him of his effectiveness before his 27th birthday.

OREL HERSHISER, RHP (1983-1994, 2000)

Like Valenzuela, Hershiser was ridden hard and then struggled. From 1984 to 1989, he averaged 242 innings per year with a 16-11 record and sparkling 2.58 ERA. For the rest of his Dodgers tenure he had a 36-38 record and 3.66 ERA, throwing 140 innings per year. His best year was 1988. He set a record with 59 consecutive scoreless innings, went 23-8 with a 2.26 ERA to win the Cy Young Award, and was MVP of both NLCS and World Series.

CLAYTON KERSHAW, LHP (2008-Present)

Great pitcher, great humanitarian. Adjusted for ballpark and scoring environment, Kershaw's career 2.43 ERA is easily the best in franchise history. He lowered his career ERA every year from 2009 to 2017, winning three Cy Young Awards and finishing in the top five four other times. At 33, he's in the downside of a first-ballot Hall of Fame career, with a sometimes-balky back, but he remains one of the game's top pitchers. The Dodgers' 2020 World Championship, with Kershaw winning two games in the World Series, is a feel-good story in a year desperate for feel-good stories.

A Taxonomy of 2020 Abnormalities

by Rob Mains

I'm going to start this with a trivia question. Trust me, it's relevant. Don't bother skipping to the end of the article to find the answer, it's not there.

Only five players have appeared in 140 or more games for 16 straight seasons. Who are they?

It's a trivia question starting off an essay, so you know how this works: Whatever you guessed, you're wrong. It's okay. As someone who purchased this book, chances are good that you're an educated baseball fan. But the circumstances behind 2020 force us to abandon, or at least seriously question, some of our favorite patterns and crutches for evaluating the game we love.

We just completed what was undoubtedly the strangest season in MLB history. No fans, geographically limited schedule, universal DH, seven-inning twin bills, runners on second in extra innings, a 16-team postseason, a club playing at a Triple-A stadium. Some of these changes will likely persist (sorry), but we've never had so many tweaks dumped on us all at once, at least not since they figured out how many balls were in a walk.

And the biggest, of course, was the 60-game season. The 19th century was dotted with teams that went bankrupt before the season ended, but the lone season with only 60 scheduled games was 1877. That year there were only six teams, the league rostered a total of 77 players (just 16 more than the 2020 Marlins), and batters called for pitches to be thrown high or low by the pitcher, who was 50 feet away. We can say the 2020 season was easily the shortest ever for recognizable baseball.

As such, it'll stand out. Few abbreviated seasons do. Just about everybody reading this knows the 1994 season ended after Seattle's Randy Johnson struck out Oakland's Ernie Young for the last out of the Mariners-A's game on August 11. The ensuing player strike wiped out the rest of the season and the postseason. Teams played only 112-117 games that year.

And many of you know that a strike in the middle of the 1981 season split the season in two, resulting in the only Division Series until 1995. Teams played only 103-111 games that year, the shortest regular season since 1885.

Those two seasons are memorable. So when we see that nobody drove in 100 runs in 1981, or that Greg Maddux was the only pitcher with 180 or more innings pitched in 1994, we think, "Of course. Strike year."

But we don't remember other short years. You might not recall that the 1994 strike spilled into the next year, chopping 18 games off the 1995 schedule. You might've read that the 1918 season, played during the last pandemic, ended after Labor Day due to the government's World War I "work or fight" order. A strike erased the first week and a half of the 1972 season, but that year's best known as the last time pitchers batted in the American League.

The point is, while we don't remember small changes to the schedule, we remember the big ones. The 1981 mid-season strike. The 1994 season- and Series-ending strike. And, of course, the pandemic-shortened 2020 season. We won't need a reminder why Marcell Ozuna's 18 homers were the fewest to lead the National League in a century. (Literally; Cy Williams led with 15 in 1920.)

Now, about that trivia question. The five players are Hank Aaron, Brooks Robinson, Pete Rose, Ichiro Suzuki, and Johnny Damon. The one nobody gets, of course, is Damon, and a lot of people miss Ichiro, whose last season of 140-plus games came garbed in the red-orange and ocean blue of Miami when he was 42. That's half of what makes it a good question. The other half is the two guys whom many think made the list but didn't. Lou Gehrig? His streak started in the Yankees' 42nd game of the 1925 season and lasted only 13 seasons after that. And everybody assumes Cal Ripken Jr. did it, having played 2,632 straight games over 17 seasons. But one of those 17 seasons was 1994, when the Orioles played only 112 games.

My point? *I just told you* everybody remembers the 1994 strike year, but everybody forgets it fell in the middle of Ripken's streak, separating the first twelve years from the last four. Just because we recall something doesn't mean it's always at the front of our minds.

Nobody is going to forget 2020, and baseball is obviously not the main reason. But there will come a time in the future when you're looking at a player's or a team's record, and there will be baffling numbers there for 2020, and you'll think, "I wonder what happened." (Not to mention the missing line for minor league players.) Just like you forgot that the 1994 strike limited Ripken to 112 games.

Try not to forget it, though. The 2020 season resulted in weird statistical results for several reasons.

There were only 60 games.

I know, duh. But that had impacts beyond counting stats like Ozuna's home run total or Yu Darvish and Shane Bieber leading the majors with eight wins. (I know, pitcher wins, but still.)

The 162-game season is the longest among major North American sports, and that duration gives us a gift. Over the course of a long season, small variations tend to even out. A player who has a ten-game hot streak will probably have a ten-game cold streak. A team that starts the year losing a bunch of close games will probably win a bunch of them. We get regression to the mean. Statistics stabilize.

Consider flipping a coin. Over the long run, we expect it to come up heads about half the time. But the fewer flips, the more variation there'll be. If you flip a coin six times, probability theory tells us you'll get at least two-third heads about 34 percent of the time. Flip it 30 times, your chance of two-thirds heads drops to five percent.

Or, relevant to this case, if you flip a coin 60 times, your chance of getting at least 36 heads—that's 60 percent—is 7.75 percent. Expand the coin-flipping to 162 times, and the chance of getting 60 percent heads drops to 0.73 percent.

In other words, the odds of an outcome that's 20 percent better (or worse) than expected is *more than ten times higher* when you flip your coin 60 times than when you do it 162 times. Call it small sample size, call lack of mean reversion, or call it luck not evening out, 162 is a lot more predictive than 60. You get much more variation over 60 games than over 162. Bieber's 1.63 ERA and 0.87 FIP aren't something we'd see over a full season, and neither is Javier Baéz's .203/.238/.360.

Some players' lines in 2020 look normal. Brian Anderson had an .811 OPS in 2019 and an .810 OPS in 2020. (He probably would have gotten that last point if he'd been given enough time.) But there are many like Bieber and Baéz, some of them from young players still establishing their talent levels. The answer to the question, "What went right or wrong for that guy in 2020?" is most likely "Nothing, it was just a 2020 thing."

Preseason training was abbreviated for hitters.
Every year, spring training drags. Players get tired of it, fans get tired of it, and you sure can tell sportswriters get tired of it. Yes, something to get everyone into shape is necessary, but does it really have to drag on for over a month? Can't we shorten it?

The 2020 season answered in the negative, at least for hitters. Warren Spahn is credited with saying that hitting is timing and pitching is upsetting timing. It appears nobody had his timing down after the abbreviated July summer camp. Through August 9—18 games into the season—MLB batters were hitting .230/.311/.395 with a .275 BABIP. That BABIP, had it held, would have been the lowest since 1968, the Year of the Pitcher. In recent years it's hovered around .300.

It didn't hold. Play returned to more normal levels the rest of the year: .249/.325/.425 with a .297 BABIP starting August 10. But batters whose play concentrated in those first two weeks wound up with ugly lines. Andrew

Benintendi went on the injured list with a season-ending rib cage strain on August 11. His final line: .103/.314/.128 in 14 games. Franchy Cordero went on the IL with a hamate bone fracture on August 9 and a .154/.185/.231 line. Even though he came back strong in a late September return, it was too late to repair his full-season numbers.

Preseason training was abbreviated for pitchers.

Every year, spring training drags. Players get tired of it, fans get tired of it … wait, I already said that. But the abbreviated preseason was tough on pitchers, too. As noted, they had the upper hand coming out of the gate. But then they lost that hand. And then their arms, too.

The 2020 season was spread over 67 days. During those 67 days, 237 pitchers hit the Injured List, compared to 135 in the first 67 days of 2019. A lot of those IL stints, though, were COVID-19-related. Still, over the first 67 days of the 2019 season, there were 72 pitchers on the IL with arm injuries. That figure jumped to 110 in 2020, a 53 percent increase.

There are a number of factors contributing to pitcher arm injuries, ranging from usage to velocity, but it appears that attenuated preseason training played a role. A lot of pitchers had super-short seasons due to arm woes. Corey Kluber, Roberto Osuna, and Shohei Ohtani combined for seven innings, none after August 8. All suffered arm injuries. We'll never know whether they'd have fared better with a longer preseason, but we can guess how they probably feel.

Everybody played.

Rosters were set to expand from 25 to 26 in 2020, so even if we'd had a normal season, we'd have likely seen 2019's record of 1,410 players on MLB rosters broken. But due to the pandemic, rosters started the year at 30 and were cut to only 28. Add multiple COVID-19 absences and the revolving door caused by poor starts by hitters and a rash of pitcher arm injuries, and 1,289 players appeared in MLB games in 2020. The comparable figure over the first 67 days of the 2019 season was 1,109. That 16 percent increase works out to an average of six more players per team in 2020 compared to a similar slice of 2019. A future look back at 2020 rosters will include a lot of unfamiliar names.

Plus became a minus.

In advanced metrics, we adjust batter and pitcher performance for park and league/era variations. A plus sign appended to the end of a measure means that it's adjusted for park and league. It's scaled to an average of 100, with higher figures above average and lower figures below average. (Similarly, a metric with a minus is also park- and league-adjusted and scaled to 100, with lower values better.) Here at BP, our advanced measure of offensive performance is DRC+. Baseball-Reference has OPS+ and FanGraphs has wRC+.

Using park and league adjustments, we can compare Dante Bichette's 1995 Steroid Era season at pre-humidor Coors Field (.340/.364/.620, 40 homers, 128 RBI, MVP runner-up) with Jim Wynn's 1968 Year of the Pitcher season at the cavernous Astrodome (.269/.376/.474, 26 homers, 67 RBI, no MVP votes). It's not close. DRC+, OPS+, and wRC+ all give the nod to Wynn, handily. This is a useful tool. As my Baseball Prospectus colleague Patrick Dubuque tweeted last fall, "Please note that when I ask how you are, I am already adjusting for era."

The 2020 season messes up plus (and minus) stats for two reasons. First, the park adjustment was based on only 30 home games instead of the usual 81. Everything noted above regarding the short season applies, literally doubly, to park effect calculations. DRC+ uses a single-season park factor. OPS+ uses a three-year average and wRC+ five years. The figure for 2020 is suspect.

Second, OPS+ and wRC+ adjust for league: American and National. (DRC+ adjusts for opponent, regardless of league.) While there were two leagues in 2020, they were an artificial construct. To reduce travel, teams played opponents geographically, not based on league. There weren't two leagues, American and National. There were three, Western, Central, and Eastern.

That makes a difference because teams in the same league played in different run-scoring environments. AL teams scored 4.58 runs per game, NL teams 4.71. That's a small difference. But teams in the East scored 0.21 more runs per game (4.95) than teams in the West (4.74), and they both scored a lot more than Central teams (4.25). Adjusting for league misses that difference, so this book will be safe in that regard, but other sources may be distorted somewhat.

Not every game was a "game."
In 2020, the rising tide of strikeouts was finally stemmed. Strikeouts per team per game fell from 8.8 in 2019 to 8.7 in 2020. That marked the first decline after 14 straight annual increases.

In 2020, the rising tide of strikeouts rose higher. Batters struck out in 23.4 percent of plate appearances compared to 23.0 percent in 2019. That marked the 15th straight annual increase.

Both are true statements.

Because of two rule changes—seven-inning doubleheaders and runners on second in extra innings—games in 2020 were unprecedented in their brevity. There were 37.0 plate appearances per game in 2020. The only years with fewer were 1904 and 1906-1909. The average game in 2020 entailed 8.61 innings pitched, the fewest since 1899.

So when you see any per-game stats for 2020, you need to increase them by 3 or 4 percent to get them on equal footing with recent years.

Or, better, just ignore them. Last year happened. There were major league games contested between major league teams. But when you're looking at those physical or electronic baseball cards, when you're weaving narratives over why this young player's inevitable rise to stardom fell apart or why that old veteran rekindled his magic, don't linger on the 2020 line. It was just too weird.

Thanks to Lucas Apostoleris for research assistance.

—Rob Mains is an author of Baseball Prospectus.

Tranches of WAR

by Russell A. Carleton

We ask "replacement level" to be a lot of things. Sometimes contradictory things. Sometimes I wonder if we know what it even means anymore. The original idea was that it represented the level of production that a team could expect to get from "freely available talent", including bench players, minor leaguers, and waiver wire pickups. It created a common benchmark to compare everyone to, and for that reason, it represented an advancement well beyond what was available at the time. In fact, it created a language and a framework for evaluating players that was not just better but *entirely* different than what came before it.

But then we started mumbling in that language. The idea behind "wins above replacement" was one part sci-fi episode and one part mathematical exercise. Imagine that a player had disappeared before the season and suddenly, in an alternate timeline, his team would have had to replace him. The distance between him and that replacement line was his value. We need to talk about that alternate timeline.

Without getting too into 2:00 am "deep conversations" with extensive navel-gazing, it's worth thinking about why one player might not be playing, while another might.

- A player might not be playing because he has a short-term injury or his manager believes that he needs a day off.
- A player might not be playing because he has a longer-term injury that requires him to be on the injured list.

There's a difference here between these two situations. In particular, the first one generally *doesn't* involve a compensatory roster move, while the second one does. It's possible, though not guaranteed, that the person who will be replacing the injured/resting player would be the same in either case. That matters. Teams generally carry a spare part for all eight position players on the diamond, although in the era of a four-player bench, those spare parts usually are the backup plan for more than one spot.

Los Angeles Dodgers 2021

A couple of years ago, I posed a hypothetical question. Suppose that a team had two players in its system fighting for a fourth outfielder spot. One of them was a league average hitter, but would be worth 20 runs below average if allowed to play center field for a full season. One of them was a perfectly average fielder, but would be 15 runs below average as a hitter, if allowed to play an entire season. Which of the two should the team roster? It's tempting to say the second one, as overall, he is the better player. That misses the point. A league average hitter on the bench isn't just a potential replacement for an injured outfielder. He might also pinch hit for the light-hitting shortstop in a key spot. You keep the average hitter on the roster, even though he isn't a hand-in-glove fit for one specific place on the field, because being a bench player is a different job description than being a long-term fill-in for someone. If you find yourself in need of a longer-term fill-in, you can bring the other guy up from AAA.

When we're determining the value of an everyday player though, if he had disappeared before the season and a team would have had to replace his production, they likely would have done it with a player who was a long-term fill-in type because they would have had to replace a guy who played everyday. Maybe that's the same guy that they would have rostered on their bench anyway, but we don't know. It gets to the query of what we hope to accomplish with WAR. Are we looking for an accurate modeling of reality or are we looking for a common baseline to compare everyone to? Both have their uses, but they are somewhat different questions.

Let's talk about another dichotomy.

- A player might not be playing because he isn't very good and is a bench-level player.
- A player might not be playing because there is another player on the team who has a situational advantage that makes him the better choice today. The classic case of this is a handedness platoon. On another day, he might be a better choice.

When we think about player usage, I think we're still stuck in the model that there are starters and there are scrubs. We have plenty of words for bench players or reserves or backups or utility guys. We do still have the word "platoon" in our collective vocabulary, but in the age of short benches, it's hard to construct one. It's always been hard to construct them. You have to find two players who hit with different hands, have skill sets that complement each other, and probably play the same position. In the era of the short bench, one of them had probably better double as a utility player in some way. Baseball has a two-tiered language geared toward the idea of regulars and reserves. The fact that it was so easy for me to find plenty of synonyms for "a player whose primary function is to come into a game to replace a regular player if he is injured or resting" should tell you something.

I'm always one to look for "unspoken words" in baseball. What is it called when someone is both half of a platoon and the utility infielder? That guy exists sometimes, but he reveals himself in that role—usually by accident. We don't have a word for that, and whenever I find myself saying "we don't have a word for that", I look for new opportunities. What do you call it, further, when the job of being the utility infielder is decentralized across the whole infield with occasional contributions from the left fielder? It's not even a "super-utility" player. What happens when you build your entire roster around the idea that everyone will be expected to be a triple major?

⚾ ⚾ ⚾

I think someone else beat me to this one, and on a grand scale. Platoons work because we know that hitters of the opposite hand to the pitcher get better results than hitters of the same hand, usually to the tune of about 20 points of OBP. If you want to express that in runs, it usually comes out to somewhere around 10 to 12 runs of linear weights value prorated across 650 PA. But hang on a second, now let's say that we have two players who might start today, both of roughly equal merit with the bat. One has a handedness advantage, but is the worse fielder of the two. In that case, as long as his "over the course of a season" projection as a fielder at whatever position you want to slot him into is less than a 10-run drop from the guy he might replace, then he's a better option today.

We're not used to thinking of utility players as bat-first options, who would play below-average defense at three different infield positions. That guy might hook on as a 2B/3B/LF type (Howie Kendrick, come on down!) but teams usually think to themselves that they need as their utility infielder someone who "can handle" shortstop, the toughest of the infield spots to play. If someone can do that *and* hit well, he's probably already starting somewhere, so he's not available as a utility infielder. It's easier for those glove guys to find a job. In a world where the replacement for a shortstop *has to be* the designated utility infielder, that makes sense.

But as we talked about last week, we're living in a different world. The rate at which a replacement for a regular starter turns out to be *another starter* shifting over to cover has gone way up over the last five years. There was always some of it in the game, but this has been a supernova of switcheroos. Now if your second baseman is capable of playing a decent shortstop, that 2B/3B/LF guy can swap in. He's not actually playing shortstop, and maybe the defense suffers from the switch, but if he's got enough of a bat, he might outhit those extra fielding miscues. And in doing so, he is effectively your backup shortstop.

Somewhere along the lines, teams got hip to the idea of multi-positional play from their regulars. I've written before about how you can't just put a player, however athletic, into a new position and expect much at first. The data tell us that. Eventually, players can learn to be multi-positionalists, but it takes time, roughly on the order of two months, before they're OK. But there's a hidden message in there. If you give a player some reps at a new spot, he's a reasonably gifted athlete and somewhat smart and willing to learn, he could probably pick it up enough to get to "good enough," and it doesn't take forever. You just have to be purposeful about it. Maybe you get to the point where you can start to say "he's still below average but we could move him there and get another bat into the lineup, and it's a net win."

Teams have started to build those extra lessons into their player development program. It used to be seen as a mark of weakness to be relegated to "utility player" because that meant that you were a bench player (all those synonyms above come with a side of stigma). Now, it's a way of building a team. If you get a few reps in the minors (where it doesn't count) at a spot, you'll have at least played the spot at game speed before. There are limits to how far you can push that. A slow-footed "he's out in left field because we don't have the DH" guy is never going to play short, but maybe your third baseman can try second base and not look like a total moose out there.

⚾   ⚾   ⚾

Back to WAR. I'd argue that the world of starters and scrubs is slowly disintegrating, for good cause. In the event that a regular starter really does go down with an injury–ostensibly, the alternate universe scenario that WAR is attempting to model–it makes the team a little more resilient to replacing him. And the good news is that you're more likely to be able to replace him with the best of the bench bunch, rather than the third-best guy, because the best guy doesn't have to be an exact positional match for the guy who got hurt. And that's what the manager would want to do. He'd want to replace that long-term production, not with an amalgam of everyone else who played that position, but with the best guy available from his reserves.

Now this is still WAR. We still want to retain the principle that we should be measuring a player, and not his teammates. We need some sort of common baseline, and despite what I just said, we'll still need some sort of amalgam. To construct that, I give to you the idea of the tranche. The word, if you've not heard it before, refers to a piece of a whole that is somehow segmented off. It's often used in finance to talk about layers of a financial instrument.

Here, I want you to consider that there are 30 starters at each of the seven non-battery positions (catchers should have their own WAR, since only a catcher can replace a catcher). We can identify them by playing time, and we can futz around with the definition a little bit if we need to. Next, among those who aren't in that starting pool, we identify the top tranche of the 30 best bench players, which I would again identify by playing time, and then the second and third and fourth and so on. If a player were to disappear, his manager would probably want to take a guy from that top tranche of the bench to replace him. In a world where even the starters can slide around the field, that becomes more feasible.

We can take a look at that top tranche and say "How many of them showed that they are able to play (first, second, etc.)?" and therefore could have directly substituted for the starter? How many of them could have been a direct substitute for our injured player? We don't know whether one of them would be on *a specific* team, but we can say that 40 percent of the time, a manager would have been able to draw from tranche 1 in filling the role, and 35 percent from tranche 2. But on tranche 1, we can also look at how many of those players played a position that could have then shifted and covered for that spot. We'd need some eligibility criteria for all of this (probably a minimum number of games played) but it would just be a matter of multiplication. Shortstop would be harder to fill, and managers would probably be dipping a little further down in the talent pool, and so replacement level would be lower, as it is now.

Doing some quick analysis, I found that the difference in just batting linear weights (haven't even gotten into running or fielding) between tranche 1 and tranche 2 in 2019 was about 6.5 runs, prorated across 650 PA. Between tranche 1 and tranche 3, it's 10.8 runs. The ability to shift those plate appearances up the ladder has some real value.

This part is important. We can also give credit to starters for the positions that they showed an ability to play, even if they didn't play them (this is the guy fully capable of playing center, but who's in a corner because the team already has a good center fielder) because he allows a team to carry a player who hits like a left fielder to functionally be the team's backup center fielder. He facilitates that movement upward among the tranches. We can start to appreciate the difference between a left fielder who would never be able to hack it in center (and the compensatory move that his team would have to make) and the left fielder who could do it, but just didn't have to very often.

Past that, you can continue to use whatever hitting and fielding and running metrics you like to determine a player's value, but when we get down to constructing that baseline, I'd argue we need a better conceptual and mathematical framework. It's going to require some more #GoryMath than we're used to, but I'd argue it's a better conceptualization of the way that MLB actually plays the game in 2020. If…y'know…MLB plays in 2020. If WAR is going to be our flagship statistic among the *acronymati*, then we need to acknowledge that it contains some old and starting-to-be-out-of-date assumptions about the game. We may need to tinker with it. Here's my idea for how.

—*Russell A. Carleton is an author of Baseball Prospectus.*

Secondhand Sport

by Patrick Dubuque

Back before time stopped, I liked to go to thrift stores. Now that I'm older, I rarely ever buy anything—I don't need much in my life, now—but I still enjoy the old familiar circuit: check to see if there are baseball cards to write about, look for board or card games to play with the kids, scan for random ironic jerseys, hit the book section. It takes ten, maybe fifteen minutes. Thrift stores are the antithesis of modern online shopping, because you don't know what they have, and you don't even really know what you want. It's junk, literal junk, stuff other people thought was worthless. That's what makes it great.

In an idealized economy, thrift stores shouldn't exist. Everybody has a living wage, and every product has a durability that exactly matches its desired life; nothing should need to be given away, no one should need to be given to. But then, thrift stores shouldn't work on a customer experience level, either. You wouldn't think an ethos of "let's make everything disorganized and hard to find" would lead to customer satisfaction, but low-budget retailers like TJ Maxx and Ross thrive on this model. People like bargain hunting as much for the hunting as the bargain; it's part of the experience, spending time as if it's a wager. There's a thrill, occasionally, in inefficiency.

In sports, the modern overuse of the word "inefficiency" is a condemnation: It insinuates that there is *an* efficiency, a correct way to be found, and that all other ways are wrong ways. It's prevalent in baseball but hardly contained to it; the lifehack, the Silicon Valley disruption are other examples of productivity creep in our daily lives. Their modern success makes plenty of sense. Maximization of resources, after all, is its own puzzle, and an industry of European board games is founded upon it. It's fun to take a system and optimize it, unravel it like a sudoku puzzle. If there's only one kind of genius, after all, there's no way anyone can fail to appreciate it.

Baseball has been hacking away at these perceived inefficiencies since its inception: platoons, bullpens, farm systems were all installed to extract more out of the tools at hand. But it's been a particular badge of the sabermetric movement, from Ken Phelps and his All-Star Team to Ricardo Rincon and the darlings of *Moneyball*. It's business, but it's also an ethos: the idea that there's treasure among the trash, something we all failed to appreciate until someone brought it to light.

It's the myth that made Sidd Finch so enticing, that fuels so many "best shape" narratives and new pitch promises. We all, athletes and unathletic sportswriters, want to believe that there's genius trapped inside us, and that it's just a matter of puzzling out the combination to unlock it. That our art, our style is the next inefficiency, waiting for our own Billy Beane. It's why we root for underdogs, and why we're excited for the Mike Tauchmans and the Eurubiel Durazos, champions of skin-deep mediocrity.

Except we aren't anymore, really. The days of "Free X" have descended beyond the ring of irony and into obscurity. There are still Xs to be freed, or at least one X, duplicated endlessly: Mike Ford, Luke Voit, Max Muncy. The undervalued one-dimensional slugger demonstrated how the game hasn't quite culturally caught up to its logical extreme. But for those who don't fit the rather spacious mold, times are grimmer. As Rob Arthur revealed several months ago, there's been a marked increase in the number of sub-replacement relievers. It's the outcome of a greater number of teams forced to play out games without the talent to win them, but it's also emblematic of the modern tendency of teams to dispose of their disposable assets, burning through cost-controlled arms the way that man chopped down forests in *The Lorax*. Stuff just isn't built to outlive their original owners anymore.

It's unsurprising, given how well-mined the market for inefficiencies has been of late. The disciples of the early analytics departments, and the disciples of those, have proliferated the league, with only a few backwater holdouts. The league has grown smarter, but every team has learned the same lesson. In fact, the phenomenon creates a peculiar kind of feedback loop: As teams value a specific subset of players or skills, prospective athletes learn to increase their own marketability by conforming themselves to the demands of their prospective employers.

And that's tragic, in the way that the extinction of animals is tragic; a certain amount of biodiversity in baseball has been lost. Shortstops hit like outfielders. Pitchers don't hit at all. Only the catchers remain idiosyncratic, thanks to the defensive demands of their position; eventually they too will be required to produce like everyone else, or they'll meet the fate of their battery mates. A perfect economy requires perfect production.

I mentioned earlier that more and more, I leave thrift stores empty-handed. It is true that I am more discerning than in the past; my bookshelves are full, and there are more streaming films than I will ever be able to watch. But there are other factors at play.

Thrift stores are, in a way, the bond markets of retail. When the economy is rough and other retailers are struggling, more people look secondhand for their products. But as recently as last year, publications were noting a reversal of the trend: Companies like Goodwill and Savers were expanding despite a strong economy. Publications credited a heightened sense of environmentalism and a rejection of cutting-edge fashion as drivers behind the increase, though the more likely answer is the modern American economy hasn't showered its favors equally, particularly among the young.

But it is more than just the economy. Baseball and thrift stores share something else in common, evident in our current conversations about re-starting the sport: They live in the gray area between public service and private enterprise. Thrift stores provide affordable necessities to lower-class citizens, and collectibles and fashion for the middle-class. Because of the success of the latter, prices have gone up across the board. Especially in terms of clothing, the middle-class flight from fashion into vintage has instead carried the aftereffects of fashion, including its costs, into a territory where people just want clothes. But there's another factor in the rise of prices, in the form of the internet.

The Goodwills of the world have grown smarter, too, employing the internet to extract full value from their detritus. Ebay, similarly, has lost much of the charm it had as a new frontier around the turn of the century. Everything has a price point now; even individual taste is no match for the algorithm, because anything rare, no matter how niche its market, is a collectible to someone.

The internet has had the same effect on thrift stores that sabermetrics has had on baseball; its equivalent to OBP was the bar scanner. As detailed in Slate, the rise of second-party stores on eBay and Amazon birthed an entire industry of used-good salespeople, armed with PDAs and scanners, buying books for three dollars to sell online for five. The author, Michael Savitz, reports earning $60,000 by working nearly 80 hours a week; he makes it clear that this is not a vocation of his choosing. It's long hours, with no real creativity or individuality, skimming the cream off of a local establishment and flipping it to someone with a little more money on the other side of the country. And once the vocation exists, the obvious question arises: why wait to put the wares out on the shelves? Why allow value to exist at all?

Nothing is ruined. Thrift stores will continue to sell polo shirts and DVDs, and baseball will continue to exist and make or lose money, depending on who you believe. But as we continue to refine our knowledge, we lose something in the conquest for efficiency, a delight born out of the unknown. The problem isn't the efficiency itself; we can't blame the booksellers, or the people sweeping freeways to collect grams of platinum from damaged catalytic converters. The problem is a system that requires this sort of profit-skimming behavior in order to feed families (or, for corporations, maximize shareholder return).

Los Angeles Dodgers 2021

In times like these, with the 2020 season on the brink and the collective bargaining agreement close behind, it can often feel like the current situation is untenable. It can't keep going like this, even if we don't know what to do about it. But as with thrift stores, there's an equally irresistible feeling that it *has* to keep going, that it would be unimaginable to not have this broken, amazing sport. Both industries exist on an invisible foundation of friction, of chaos and unpredictability, even as both see their foundations buffed down to a perfect, untouchable polish. But if COVID-19 and its financial ramifications do, as some have suggested, make it such that the baseball that returns is fundamentally different than the baseball that came before, perhaps this is the time to lean in, and change the game even more. Fix bunting. Make defense more difficult. Create viable, alternate strategies. Add some chaos back into baseball. It's fun when no one knows quite where things are.

—Patrick Dubuque is an author of Baseball Prospectus.

Steve Dalkowski Dreaming

by Steven Goldman

We dream of being a pitcher, of starring in the major leagues. Depending on your age and your sense of historical perspective, you might imagine yourself as Walter Johnson, throwing harder than anyone else—hitting more batters than anyone else, too, but always feeling bad about it. You could picture yourself as a Tom Seaver or a David Cone, with all the stuff in the world but still being cerebral about it, thinking about so much more than burning 'em in there. There are so many models one could choose: You could be a Lefty Gomez, Jim Bouton, or Bill Lee, skilled, but not taking the whole thing too seriously, or a Lefty Grove, Bob Gibson, or Steve Carlton, powerful but treating each start like a mission to be survived instead of a game to be enjoyed.

Very few would dream of being Steve Dalkowski, the former Baltimore Orioles prospect who died of COVID-19 last week at the age of 80. Yet, there is something just as noble in Dalkowski's negative accomplishments—and accomplishments is what they are—as there is in the precision-engineered pitching of a Greg Maddux. You have to be very good to be that bad. Dalkowski had all of the stuff of the greatest pitchers but none of the command; his story is not one of failing to conquer his limitations, but striving against one of the cruelest hands that fate or genetics or personality can deal us: A desire to achieve great things which is almost but not quite matched by the ability to meet that goal.

As with Johnson, Grove, Bob Feller, and the rest of the hard-throwing pitchers who played before the advent of modern radar guns, we have to take the word of the players and coaches who saw Dalkowski pitch as to his velocity. He was a hard-drinking, maximum-effort pitcher who, if their memories are to be believed, consistently threw over 100 miles per hour. His was the Maltese Fastball, the stuff that dreams are made of. The problem is that velocity without command and control is still a good distance from utility. Dalkowski was the most effective towel you could design for a fish, the sleekest bathing suit intended to be worn by an astronaut, but that doesn't mean he wasn't beautiful: We can appreciate a journey even if it doesn't end at the intended destination.

Whether because of sloppy mechanics he couldn't calm, an inability to understand that a consistent 98 in the strike zone would likely be more effective than a consistent 110 out of it, or all that beer, Dalkowski could never make the adjustments that pitchers like Feller and Nolan Ryan made before him, possibly because he had so far to go: Feller, who never pitched in the minors, came up at 17 and spent three years walking almost seven batters per nine innings before settling in at 3.8 beginning when he was 20. Ryan started out walking over six batters per nine but gradually improved as his long career played out; for him to go from 6.2 walks per nine with the 1966 Greenville Mets to 3.7 with the 1989 Texas Rangers represents a 40 percent reduction. An equivalent improvement by Dalkowski would still have left him walking over 11 batters per nine innings.

Dalkowski was like *The Room* of pitchers, a player so bad he became good again. Cal Ripken, Sr., who both played with and managed Dalkowski, recalled in a 1979 *Sporting News* "where are they now" piece the occasion when the pitcher crossed up his catcher and his fastball, "hit the plate umpire smack in the mask. The mask broke all to pieces and the umpire wound up in the hospital for three days with a concussion. If they ever had a radar gun in those days, I'll bet Dalkowski would have been timed at 110 miles an hour."

Signed by the Orioles out of New Britain High in Connecticut in 1957, Dalkowski was sent to Kingsport in the Appalachian League, where he pitched 62 innings. He allowed only 22 hits in 62 innings, or 3.2 per nine, a number with no equivalent in major league history (though Aroldis Chapman came close in 2014), and also struck out 121 (17.6 per nine) and walked 129 (18.7). He was also charged with 39 wild pitches. That June, one of his fastballs clipped a Dodgers prospect named Bob Beavers and carried away part of his ear. "The first pitch was over the backstop, the second pitch was called a strike, I didn't think it was," Beavers said last year. "The third pitch hit me and knocked me out, so I don't remember much after that. I couldn't get in the sun for a while, and I never did play baseball again." Former minor leaguer Ron Shelton based the *Bull Durham* pitcher Nuke LaLoosh on Dalkowski. And yet, to see him as a figure of fun, an amusing loser, is to misunderstand something unique and strange.

Dalkowski kept on posting some of the strangest lines in baseball history. Pitching for the Stockton Ports of the Class C California League in 1960, he struck out 262 and walked 262 in 170 innings. Yet, he did improve, especially after pitching for Earl Weaver at Elmira in 1962. Weaver had previously had Dalkowski at Aberdeen in 1959, but wasn't ready to grapple with him then. This time he was. "I had grown more and more concerned about players with great physical abilities who could not learn to correct certain basic deficiencies no matter how much you instructed or drilled them," he related in his autobiography, *It's What You Learn After You Know It All That Counts*. He got permission from the Orioles to give all of his players the Stanford-Binet IQ test. "Dalkowski finished in the 1 percentile in his ability to understand facts. Steve, it was said to say, had the ability to do everything but learn." [sic]

IQ tests are problematic diagnostic tools, so take Weaver's estimate of Dalkowski's mental capabilities with a grain of salt. What's important is that even if he got to the right answer by way of the wrong reason, Weaver had learned something valuable. His insight was to stop asking Dalkowski to learn new pitches and just let him get by with the two that he had. Were Dalkowski a prospect today, that would have been a no-brainer: Can't develop a third pitch? The bullpen is right over there, sir. Player development wasn't like that then, but Weaver, temporarily Dalkowski's mentor, could let him work with what he had. According to Weaver, the pitcher responded: "In the final 57 innings he pitched that season Dalkowski gave up 1 earned run, struck out 110 batters, and walked only 11." It's not true—as per the *Elmira Star-Gazette*, as of late July, Dalkowski had walked 71 in 106 innings and finished with 114 in 160 innings, which means Dalkowski's control actually faded at the end of the season rather than improved—but that doesn't mean it didn't happen in some sense, just that it didn't happen that way. Again, it's the journey, not the destination, and his ERA was 3.04 so *something* had gone right.

Also along the way: The next spring, Orioles manager Billy Hitchcock was rooting for Dalkowski to make the team as a long-man—maybe Weaver had gotten through to him. There were things out of Weaver's control, like the universe's twisted sense of humor: that March, Dalkowski's elbow went "twang."

You sometimes read that it was the Orioles' insistence on Dalkowski learning the curve that did him in, but even if they hadn't learned their lesson, the injury was probably just a coincidence: Dalkowski had thrown an incredible number of pitches over the previous few years. Still, it testifies to the dangers of trying to get what you want and risking the loss of what you had. Dalkowski tried to come back, but the 110-mph stuff was gone. A pitcher with no control and no stuff is...a civilian. What followed were years of vagabond living, arrests for drunkenness. There were Alcoholics Anonymous meetings, assistance from baseball alumni associations, but none of it took. From the 1990s until the time of his passing he dwelt in an assisted living facility, suffering from alcohol-related dementia. He'd been a heavy drinker since his teenage years. As with all those pitches per game, there was a price to be paid. You make choices on the journey and some of them are irrevocable. It's like a fairy tale: "Bite of poison apple? Don't mind if I do."

In the aforementioned *Sporting News* profile, Chuck Stevens, the head of the Association of Professional Ballplayers of America, a ballplayer charity, said, "I've got nothing against drinking. I do it myself sometimes. But, I don't condone common drunkenness. We went through lots of heartache and many dollars, but Dalkowski didn't want to help himself and we weren't going to keep him drunk." The journey is *un*like a fairy tale: No one will come along and kiss it better, not if they're busy forming judgments.

In the end, we are left with a sort of philosophical chicken/egg conundrum: Is failing to meet your goals evidence of unfulfilled potential or the lack of it? Isn't what you did by definition what you were capable of doing? Or could you have broken through to something better with the right help, the right lucky break? These are unanswerable questions, and how we try to answer them may say more about us than about the people we're judging.

No pitcher ever has it easy. *All* pitchers must work hard. *All* pitchers must refine their craft. It's almost never just about *stuff*. Dalkowski dreaming is no insult to the great pitchers who made it; from Pete Alexander to Max Scherzer, they have all earned their way up. And yet, if it is true that we can only do as much as we can do, then the journey would be more of an adventure, the ultimate triumph or defeat more noble, if like Dalkowski we lacked 100 percent of the confidence, the command, the self-possession, the commitment, the resistance to making bad decisions that so many great players possess—to be gloriously human. Or, to put it more succinctly, it would be fun to be able to throw as hard as any person ever has. Even if just for a moment, and even if nothing more came of it than that, no one could say you hadn't lived life to the fullest.

—*Steven Goldman is an author of Baseball Prospectus.*

A Reward For A Functioning Society

by Cory Frontin and Craig Goldstein

On July 5, Nationals reliever Sean Doolittle said in the middle of a press conference regarding the restart of Major League Baseball and what would later be known as summer camp, "sports are like the reward of a functioning society." This sentence was amidst a much longer, thoughtful reply about the societal and health conditions under which MLB players were being brought back. It's a very similar sentiment to one Jane McManus used on April 7, when she discussed the White House's meeting with sports commissioners. She said "sports are the effect of a functioning society—not the precursor."

Both versions of the same sentiment spoke to a laudable ideal in the context of a country that was not addressing a rampaging virus, and opting instead to bring sports back for the feeling of normalcy rather than the reality of it. "Priorities," as McManus said.

On Wednesday, the NBA's Milwaukee Bucks conducted a wildcat/political strike, refusing to come out for Game 5 of their playoff series against the Orlando Magic. The Magic refused to accept the forfeit, and shortly thereafter other playoff series were threatened by player strikes. Eventually the league moved to postpone that day's games, folding to players leveraging their united power.

The backdrop against which these actions took place was the shooting by police of Jacob Blake. Blake was shot in the back seven times by police, as he attempted to get into his vehicle. He managed to survive the assault, but is paralyzed from the waist down.

⚾ ⚾ ⚾

The step taken to walk out, first by the Milwaukee Bucks, then subsequently by other NBA, WNBA, and MLB teams, was a step toward upholding the virtue of the sentiment described by McManus and Doolittle. But that sentiment does not align with the broad history of sports in this and other countries, a history that contradicts the core of the idealistic statement.

Sports have been a significant part of American society for most of its existence, expanding in importance and influence in recent years. The idea that society was functioning in a way that was worthy of the reward of sports for most of that time is laughable. Much of America is not functioning and has not functioned for Black people, full stop. The oppressed people at the center of this political act by players, specifically Black players, in concert throughout the NBA and in fits and starts throughout Major League Baseball, have not known a society that functions for them rather than *because* of them.

Politics has been part of the sports landscape since the inception of sport, but for just about as long people have bemoaned its presence. Sports are to be an escape, it is said. An escape from what, though? A functioning society?

No, the presence of sports has never signified a cultural or political system that is on the up and up. Rather, the presence of sports *reflect and reinforce the society* that produces them.

⚾ ⚾ ⚾

The Negro Leagues were born out of societal dysfunction. The need for entirely separate leagues, composed of Black and Latino players barred from the Major Leagues because of racism? That is not a functioning society, and yet there were sports.

Even the integration of players from the Negro Leagues resulted in a transfer of power and wealth from Black-owned businesses and communities and into white ones, mirroring the dysfunction that had bled into every aspect of American society at the time. Japheth Knopp noted in the Spring 2016 Baseball Research Journal:

> *The manner in which integration in baseball—and in American businesses generally—occurred was not the only model which was possible. It was likely not even the best approach available, but rather served the needs of those in already privileged positions who were able to control not only the manner in which desegregation occurred, but the public perception of it as well in order to exploit the situation for financial gain. Indeed, the very word integration may not be the most applicable in this context because what actually transpired was not so much the fair and equitable combination of two subcultures into one equal and more homogenous group, but rather the reluctant allowance—under certain preconditions—for African Americans to be assimilated into white society.*

To understand the value of a movement, though, is not to understand how it is co-opted by ownership, but to know the people it brings together and what they demand. When Jackie Robinson—the player who demarcated the inevitability of the end of the Negro leagues—attended the March on Washington for Jobs and Freedom in 1963, he did so with his family and marched alongside the people. He stood alongside hundreds of thousands to fight for their common civil and labor rights. "The moral arc of the universe is long," many freedom fighters have echoed, "but it bends towards justice." The bend, it is less frequently said, happens when a great mass of people place the moral arc of the universe on their knee and apply force, as Jackie, his family, and thousands of others did that day.

⚾   ⚾   ⚾

Of course, taking the moral arc of the universe down from the mantle and bending it is not without risk. Perhaps the outsized influence of athletes is itself a mark of a dysfunctional society, but, nonetheless, hundreds of athletes woke up on Wednesday morning with the power to bring in millions of dollars in revenues. That very power, as we would come to find out, was matched with the equal and opposite power to *not* bring those revenues. That power, in hands ranging from the Milwaukee Bucks, to Kenny Smith in the *Inside the NBA* Studio, from the unexpected ally, Josh Hader, and his largely white teammates to the notably Black Seattle Mariners, would be exercised for a single demand: the end to state violence against Black people. Not unlike the March itself, it sat at the intersection of the civil rights of Black Americans and bold labor action. The March on Washington stood in the face of a false notion of integration—against an integration of extraction but not one of equality—and proposed something different. Just the same, the acts of solidarity of August 26, 2020 will be remembered in stark defiance of MLB's BLM-branded, but ultimately empty displays on opening weekend.

Bold defiance like this can never be without risk. By choosing to exercise this power, the Milwaukee Bucks took a risk. They risked vitriol and backlash from those they disagreed with. They risked fines or seeing their contracts voided, as a walkout like this is prohibited by their CBA. They risked forfeiting a playoff game, one that, as the No. 1 seed in the playoffs, they'd worked all year to attain. They didn't know how Orlando would respond. It wasn't clear that other teams throughout the league would follow suit in solidarity. And it wasn't known the league would accept these actions and moderately co-opt them by "postponing" games that would have featured no players.

If the league reschedules the games, some of the athletes' risk—their shared sacrifice—will be diminished, in retrospect. But they did not know any of that when they took that risk. And it is often left to athletes to take these risks when others in society won't, especially those of their same socioeconomic status and levels of influence.

It is athletes, specifically BIPOC athletes, that take them, though, because they live with the risk of being something other than white in this country every day. They are no strangers to the realities of police brutality. It seems incongruous then, to say that sports are a reward for a functioning society when we rely on athletes to lead us closer to being a functioning society. Luckily, our beloved athletes, WNBA players first and foremost among them, understand what sports truly are: a pipebender for the moral arc of the universe.

—Craig Goldstein is editor in chief of Baseball Prospectus. Cory Frontin is an author of Baseball Prospectus.

Index of Names

Alexander, Scott	36	Lee, C.C.	83
Amaya, Jacob	70, 93	Lux, Gavin	74
Barnes, Austin	16	May, Dustin	58
Bauer, Trevor	38	McGee, Jake	60
Beaty, Matt	71	McKinstry, Zach	75, 95
Beeter, Clayton	79, 94	Miller, Bobby	84, 91
Bellinger, Cody	18	Muncy, Max	22
Betts, Mookie	20	Pages, Andy	95
Buehler, Walker	40	Peters, DJ	75
Busch, Michael	72, 90	Pollock, AJ	24
Carrillo, Gerardo	80, 93	Price, David	84
Cartaya, Diego	72, 90	Ravelo, Rangel	76
Ferguson, Caleb	42	Reks, Zach	77
Gonsolin, Tony	44	Ríos, Edwin	26
González, Victor	46	Ruiz, Keibert	78, 88
Graterol, Brusdar	48	Santana, Dennis	62
Gray, Josiah	80, 87	Seager, Corey	28
Grove, Michael	95	Smith, Will	30
Hoese, Kody	73, 92	Taylor, Chris	32
Jackson, Andre	81, 92	Treinen, Blake	64
Jansen, Kenley	50	Turner, Justin	34
Kahnle, Tommy	82	Urías, Julio	66
Kelly, Joe	52	Vargas, Miguel	79, 89
Kershaw, Clayton	54	Vesia, Alex	68
Knack, Landon	94	Vogel, Jake	79, 95
Knebel, Corey	56	White, Mitch	85, 95

For the Joy of Keeping Score

THIRTY81 Project is an ongoing graphic design project focused on the ballparks of baseball. Since being established in 2013, scorecards have been a fundemantal part of the effort. Each two-page card is uniquely ballpark-centric — there are 30 variants — and designed with both beginning and veteran scorekeepers in mind. Evolving over the years with suggestions from fans, broadcasters, and official scorers, the sheets are freely available to everyone as printable letter-size PDFs at the project webshop: www.THIRTY81Project.com

Download, Print, Score, Repeat ...

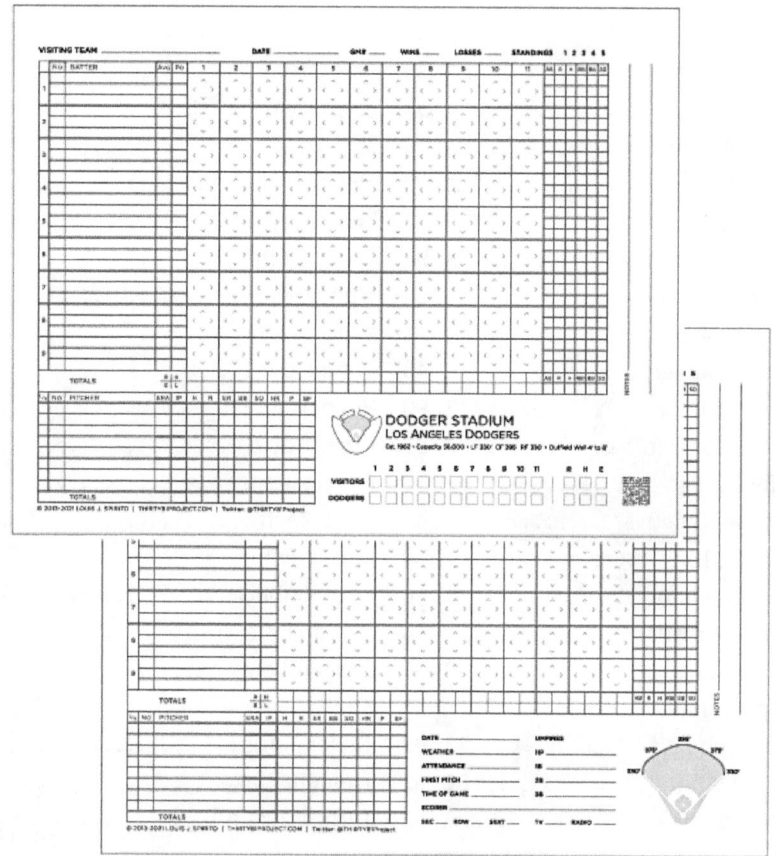

Scorecard design ©2013-2021 Louis J. Spirito | THIRTY81Project